The Four Pillars
of
Christianity

Essential Knowledge for Every Christian

Wade Smith, PhD
and
Kevin McKee, D. Min.

ISBN 978-1-64458-957-1 (paperback)
ISBN 978-1-64458-958-8 (digital)

Christian Faith Publishing, Inc.
832 Park Avenue
Meadville, PA 16335
www.christianfaithpublishing.com

Unless otherwise indicated, Scripture referenced in this book is from the New International Version (NIV) by International Bible Society. All passages were retrieved electronically from Bible Gateway: https://www.biblegateway.com

Printed in the United States of America

This book is dedicated to our families and to all the people
who have ever wondered if their faith was reasonable.

Contents

Introduction

The Threat to the Western Church

Perhaps as many as ten thousand churches have closed their doors in recent years, and up to 80 percent of the formerly churched indicate a weak belief in God. A common response from those who have left the church is that they cannot get their questions answered in a safe environment. And to throw one more rock on the pile, between 2010 and 2012, more than 50 percent of the churches added not one new member.[1]

Facts like these point to the inescapable conclusion that the influence of the church on modern culture is shrinking.[2] Small groups and well-honed praise teams will not change these trends because they are all geared toward folks who are already in church. Even well-done sermons that address spiritual growth will likely be insufficient since the foundations for those sermons are lost on many

---

[1] http://www.huffingtonpost.com/steve-mcswain/why-nobody-wants-to-go-to_b_4086016.html. The HuffPost reported on the trends associated with the lack of church attendance; http://www.christianpost.com/news/survey-reasons-why-people-leave-the-church-22882/; https://www.youtube.com/watch?v=DdbrjUp89WM&feature=youtube. Commentary on these issues had been provided by J. P. Moreland. A short synopsis can be found in this link.

[2] http://www.gallup.com/poll/155690/Confidence-Organized-Religion-Low-Point.aspx. Gallup has noted the trend in declining confidence in religion as evidenced by their 2012 report; http://churchleaders.com/pastors/pastor-articles/139575-7-startling-facts-an-up-close-look-at-church-attendance-in-america.html. As sobering as the reported trends are, they may actually be incorrectly optimistic, perhaps overestimating attendance by more than 50 percent.

a skeptic. If the church in America is to reinvigorate itself, we believe it will be necessary to reclaim the high ground for the intellectual defense of our beliefs.

Consider the thoughts provided below.

Modern culture is a tremendous force. It impacts all classes of society. It affects the ignorant as well as the learned. What is to be done about it? In the first place, the church may simply withdraw from the conflict. She may simply allow the mighty stream of modern thought to flow by unheeded and do her work merely in the back eddies of the current. There are still some men in the world who have been unaffected by modern culture. They may still be won for Christ without intellectual labor. And they must be won. It is useful; it is necessary work. If the church is satisfied with that alone, let her give up the scientific education of her ministry. Let her assume the truth of her message and learn simply how it can be applied to modern industrial and social conditions. Let her give up the laborious study of Greek and Hebrew. Let her abandon the scientific study of history to the men of the world. In a day of increased scientific interest, let the Church go on becoming less scientific. In a day of increased specialization, of renewed interest in philology and in history, of more rigorous scientific method, let the Church go on abandoning her Bible to her enemies. They will study it scientifically, rest assured, if the Church does not. Let her substitute sociology altogether for Hebrew, practical experiences for the proof of the gospel. Let her shorten the preparation of her ministry, let her permit it to be interrupted more and more by premature practical activity. By doing so, she will win a straggler here and there. But her winnings will be but temporary. The great current of modern culture will engulf her puny eddy. God will save her somehow—out of the depths. But the labor of centuries will have been swept away. God grant that the church may not resign herself to that.

The article goes on to say the following:

During the last thirty years, there has been a tremendous defection from the Christian Church. It is evidenced even by things that lie on the surface. For example, by the decline in church attendance and in Sabbath observance and in the number of candidates for the ministry. Special explanations, it is true, are sometimes given for these discouraging tendencies. But why should we deceive ourselves; why comfort ourselves by palliative explanations? Let us face the facts. The falling off in church attendance, the neglect of Sabbath observance—these things are simply surface indications of a decline in the power of Christianity. Christianity is exerting a far less powerful direct influence in the civilized world today than it was exerting thirty years ago.[3]

If you did not do so the first time, reread the above excerpts carefully. They provide a compelling analysis of the church and its place in society today, except that the words were written in 1913 by J. Gresham Machen for the *Princeton Theological Review*. The words may be over a century old, but the thoughts succinctly crystallize the position the church finds itself in today. Increasingly, we find our-

---

[3] https://theologymix.com/church-life/christianity-and-culture-gresham-machen. The quote from Machen is taken from his work in the *Princeton Review*. It is highly recommended reading. Machen's name may not be familiar to you, but his legacy is enduring as he was one of the primary founders of the Orthodox Presbyterian Church.

selves in a culture that, at its heart, is hell-bent on marginalizing the church and minimizing its relevance until it and its worldview are tossed on the trash heap of similarly discredited beliefs. There is a battle raging to establish and maintain the high ground of truth, and the church cannot afford to hold back anything that supports its position.

This book is an effort to equip the church to effectively answer a culture that grows increasingly hostile to the church's claims. The church must be able to defend its core beliefs and, accordingly, its core behaviors. The core beliefs we refer to here are straightforward: (1) the existence of the God of the Bible, (2) Jesus is the divine Son of God, (3) Jesus resurrected from the grave, and (4) the Christian perspective on suffering and evil is rational.

Absent adequate defenses of these pillars of the Christian faith, the Christian has only one thing to offer a skeptic—their personal testimony. Indeed, any life changed by the regenerative power of the Holy Spirit is a story worth telling, but will that be sufficient in today's culture? If Machen were alive, he would argue that it was not true in his time, and he would undoubtedly assert that it is not true today either.

Defended well, the pillars of the church assure everyone that the church and its cause are legitimate. And if the church is legitimate, then it is correct to argue that it is the vehicle God uses to provide a source of hope to a world desperately seeking something that can be trusted as true. We fear that many Christians are low level consumers (i.e., they are unable to adequately articulate a defense for their beliefs). If that is the case, then they are unprepared to give an answer for the hope that they have (1 Peter 3:15).

Machen focuses on the role of the seminary in preparing ministers to be effective defenders of Christ, and that makes sense since his intended audiences were seminaries. Still, it is easy to generalize his thoughts to the laity as well. The Great Commission cannot be realized without the body of Christ's participation. Speaking to others about the hope that we hold is not something assigned specifically to pastors. In fact, nothing can be further from the truth. It is the responsibility of every person who has been changed by receiving Christ to always be prepared to give an account for why they believe. We trust God that this book will be a useful tool toward this end.

Chapter 1

Why This Book and Why Right Now?

> My faith was paralyzed for five years because I
> did not know how to answer these questions.[1]

This book is the result of many conversations about the current state of the church. We are writing primarily to and for believers, with a couple of immediate thoughts in mind:

- First, we are convinced that too many believers live out their faith with insufficient assurances for the truth of their beliefs. In other words, it may be said that they hope their beliefs are true instead of knowing that to be the case. If we are correct, many believers understandably compartmentalize their faith and keep it secret because they are not convinced it can withstand scrutiny.

- Second, if we are correct and there are too many believers that find themselves paralyzed, then the inevitable result will be marginally effective Christians and churches. Believers affected by incertitude are not apt to lead radically changed lives that demonstrate that God is the ulti-

---

[1] The quote is from a longtime believer who harbored doubts for years. When asked why she did not seek answers for her questions, she said: "I didn't think anyone had the answers."

mate reality and that Jesus Christ, God made man, is the only means to that ultimate reality. It would be naive to think believers of this sort will be able to speak well of their Lord. It is also naive to think that marginalized Christians will flock to this book or to any other book of this nature. Equipping such believers, therefore, will almost certainly fall to churches and their leadership.

- Finally, we live in an increasingly relativistic and postmodern world where absolutes and reason no longer form the basis of many people's thinking. Experience and feelings are highly valued today. While these aspects of life and living are important, they inevitably shift. Without an assurance of belief, many Christians feel that their faith is shifting and unstable. They are unable to stand firmly on their own faith, and therefore they cannot and do not help others to understand why the Christian claims are true.

We write to provide the believer with assurances that their faith is rational and their hope is secure. Believers equipped with this knowledge are able to put on the full armor of Christ and speak about what they believe with grace and humility. In case you haven't noticed, popular culture demonstrates an ever-growing tendency to question Christianity, so there is a real need to armor up.

Although it is true that Christianity as a faith is being questioned, such a statement by itself is almost meaningless because Christianity means so many different things to so many skeptics. In other words, we as the church have not done an adequate job of defining exactly what Christianity is and exactly why these beliefs are foundational, grounded, and rational. As a result, the church seems to be on its heels in the culture wars. Instead of defining the conversation, we are being forced to react to the ever-increasing attacks against Christianity. That need not happen. If we possess truth, then truth should be the starting point for our faith and indeed for our lives. A long time ago, a Roman governor asked a great question: "What is truth?" We hope to provide an answer.

Who Are We?

At the core of Christianity, three central tenets undergird all other facets of the faith. We will refer to them as the pillars of Christianity. These pillars, in our view, represent absolutes for the faith. In other words, without these pillars, there is no Christianity:

- The God of the Bible exists.
- Jesus Christ is divine.
- Christ resurrected from the tomb.

In addition to these three pillars, there is one more necessary component to Christianity. We must be able to provide a rational answer to the problem of evil and suffering in our world. Failure to do so leaves untold numbers of people in desolate desperation with no hope for the future and no assurance that they are loved by the God of the Bible. Therefore, when we refer to the pillars of Christianity throughout this book, we intend the term to include all four points.

Internal Conversations

Christians like to argue, and this dates back to the early church that had so many matters to settle that the leaders created a church council to hold court on doctrinal issues. You can read Acts 15 for a glimpse into these early workings. Christians of today are often quite ready to carry on internal debates about the age of the earth, perseverance of the saints, predestination, God's sovereignty versus free will, infant baptism, and on and on. Each of these conversations has a place at the table at some point, but none of them matter a whit if the pillars of Christianity are not true.

We often spend our time speaking with skeptics about topics that are not directly connected to the pillars. That means conversations get very confused and the skeptic has every right to point out that the church itself cannot agree on these matters. So why should he or she worry about what church folk have to say at all? It is important to separate conversations about *doctrines* from conversations about *foundations*. The foundational pillars of Christianity are independent of denominations, and they should provide the starting point for conversations about Christianity.

Although listed separately, the arguments are all tightly connected. Christ's resurrection speaks to his divinity as well as to the existence of God, for example. But skeptics may not be comfortable starting with that argument and may note that they see no evidence for God. If that is the case, they will likely not take the subsequent claims of Christianity seriously.

Skeptical arguments against Christianity's pillars tend to come from three arenas: science, history, and morality. As noted, arguments from science tend to focus on God's existence. Historical arguments usually attack the veracity and reliability of scripture. Moral arguments tend to be philosophical and question how an all-powerful, all-loving God can allow evil to flourish. Within these camps, there are smaller camps. But in general, these three areas are where most skeptical objections are generated.

Objectives and Applications

Our aim is that when you finish this book, you will have a foundation of knowledge that is reassuring to your own spiritual walk with God. This knowledge will also be useful when you engage skeptics in conversation. In addition, the topics in this book are relevant to churches seeking to lay strong foundations for their congregations, so they can be spiritually grounded and actively engaged in spreading the good news of Jesus. All that said, we are not trying to create a magnum opus of apologetics. In this sense, the book is adequate but not exhaustive. Those wishing to delve deeper into any of these topics will find a wealth of written material that will challenge them even further.

The applications for this knowledge are therefore both personal and corporate. First, we hope that you, the reader, benefit from the information in this book. Second, we want to challenge churches to begin to think about the issues we raise and how those issues relate to their congregations. Specifically, we want churches to actively assess whether their congregations are generally equipped to defend their faith and rely on their faith when circumstances warrant. Our own experiences tell us that many churches will likely find their congregations ill prepared to address the rising skepticism and derision among the general population.

We are also challenging churches to revisit the attention given to the pillars of Christianity and to their documentation of God's power to provide eternal life, through Jesus Christ, to all those who believe. Being able to express these realities and then act accordingly sends a powerful message to a hurting world where suffering is all too common. If we do not behave consistent with our message, then we are no more than mere mouthpieces that spout truth but never act on it. The skeptic will smell out this type of hypocrisy from a mile away.

Finally, we also want to provide individuals with one source that can speak to these issues collectively. As we noted, we are not trying to provide exhaustive analyses for any of these topics. Our goal is to promote general expertise, expertise sufficient to equip the believer with the full armor of God (Ephesians 6) so that he or she can stand up for their faith in confident humility.

As Americans, we should all know "The Star-Spangled Banner" and the Pledge of Allegiance because their messages are inextricably bound to being an American. As Christians, we should all know and be able to communicate rational and biblical arguments for the pillars because their messages are likewise inextricably bound to the Christian obligation to be the hands and feet of Christ.

A Rude Awakening

If the pillars of the faith are foundational, then church members should be able to provide rational defenses for them. That said, we wondered what might happen in the average church if members were asked to write down all they know about the following four questions: What is the evidence for God's existence? How do we know Christ is divine? What is the evidence for the resurrection? Why does an all-loving, all-powerful God allow suffering?

We began by asking a pastor with over forty years of experience, a former member of the Billy Graham evangelism team, and a true man of God with encyclopedic biblical recall, what he thought would happen if we asked these questions to all the attendees of the church he founded over forty years ago. He was quick to respond that it would not be pretty; he was confident that most would not know what to write.

We followed up by asking about one hundred people in our own church through focus groups and apologetics classes what their opinion would be for the general congregational response to the questions. Once again, the answers were not very optimistic, with the typical response suggesting that 10 percent would be able to respond and the most positive suggesting around 25 percent. One respondent said he felt like he could answer the questions, but then he went on to say he did not actually learn any of the material in church. Another response was from a former church elder with an extensive church history. He was succinct: "It would be bloody."

This begs a question: Are these results typical of other churches, or are they isolated responses from one particular church? What we discovered strongly suggests that this inability to offer explanations to these questions is not isolated at all.

Recently, a class was held about the four pillars of the faith. It was attended by Pentecostals, Baptists, nondenominationals, charismatics, and a couple of skeptics. The average age of the attendees was above forty and there were about thirty-five people present. Collectively, there was a lot of church history in the room, with most reporting they had been nearly lifelong church attendees. Everyone had attended more than one church and several had attended about five churches. We estimated that there were well over one hundred churches, both past and present, represented at the meeting. And this setting provided an excellent opportunity to pose the question and ask people to respond not only for the church they were currently attending but also for all the churches they had ever attended.

You can probably guess by now that the results were nearly identical to the responses that had been given by the one hundred or so folks who had already responded. In short, there was not one person who stated that they had any confidence that the average attendee at any church they had attended would be able to write much of anything about these seminal issues.

Chew on that one for a while, and then reflect on your own experiences in all the churches you have ever attended. Now ask yourself this question: How do we as Christians speak to others about Christ as Messiah or Christ as the conqueror of death if we cannot speak to the divinity of Christ and the proof of his resurrection? Can it be that the reason so many people are nervous when speaking about their personal beliefs is that, for the most part, that is exactly what they are? Can it be that many Christians hold valid beliefs but do not appreciate the rational basis for those beliefs? Or worse yet, can they have little to no rational basis for their belief? It is one thing to hope what you believe is true, and it is entirely another matter to be convinced that what you believe is true. We are concerned that there are too many in the pews who base their beliefs on things they *hope* are true rather than things they *know* are true.

If this is the case, it will go a long way toward explaining why churches are increasingly swapping members and why most churches are harbors for folks who have left other churches. Folks may very well be looking for reasons that justify their beliefs in the churches they attend. If church A does not deliver, try church B.

It will also help to explain reluctance to engage skeptics. We have all been sensitized to the mind-set that personal beliefs are, for lack of a better word, personal. What you believe is your business, and what I believe is mine. This type of thinking assumes there is no belief that is a better belief. Or if there is a better belief, the only way to reach that belief is through personal experience. Take that thinking and extend it to a believer who cannot readily identify why their beliefs are solid, and it is easy to see how the believer will rarely, if ever, engage a skeptic and follow Peter's charge to give an account of why he believes.

When we do engage skeptics, we tend to do so with a one size fits all mentality. But as you will soon see from our own life stories, one size definitely does not fit all. In fact, it would not be far-fetched to look at our stories as anchors for a continuum where the head is on one side and the heart is on the other. If you do that, it becomes clear that there is no single tactic that can be used to speak to a skeptic. We will develop that theme later in the book. First, let's take a look at our two personal stories.

Two Decidedly Different Stories
Connecting the Head and the Heart

Kevin's Story

Everyone's story of how Jesus found and saved them is different and varied. Wade's story and mine are indeed different. I grew up in a family that was churchgoing when I was young. But by the time I was an adolescent, it wasn't. During those turbulent years, I ventured into the seventies world of drugs, sex, and rock and roll. Because our home was suburban in nature, this wasn't a ridiculously rebellious season. I had a loving and stable home, which made life more constant than other teens in rebellion. Yet even though those years might be considered tame, my middle school and high school exploits left me full of guilt and shame.

I didn't know anything about Jesus, but I knew that if he did exist, as I understood him to be, he wouldn't approve of my choices.

I also struggled with severe learning disabilities. In the seventies, not much was known about dyslexia. Its overall effect on me was to greatly affect my reading ability and to leave me feeling stupid a lot of the time. School was difficult for me and took great effort.

There are basically three hurdles we all face—intellectual, emotional, and volitional. Within these hurdles, some tend to be larger than others. For me, the largest hurdle was emotional. I'm basically a very relational person, and I feel things deeply. I don't know if my learning disabilities contributed to this, but I believe they did. So when I came to understand Jesus, there wasn't an intellectual hurdle to overcome. For me, the hurdle was emotional.

God helped me overcome this hurdle by providing a loving community, a family. This community had joy and seemed to generally be void of the isolating effects that are caused by shame and guilt. They had the authenticating mark of love. And they shared this love lavishly. This, and an opportunity to hear and respond to the gospel, forever changed me.

As I grew in Jesus, the peace of God and the love of God filled me though the Holy Spirit. This gave me confidence. However, sleeping within me was a desire to know more. At that time, I was not really sensitive to the desire. As time went on though, the desire awakened and it was strong. I spent four years mining for understanding while searching for the reasonable side of faith in seminary. While this knowledge was very helpful to me, what made it critically importantly was the ability to share it.

While I came to Jesus through my heart first, I met many people, friends, and family who started with their head first. So I knew I needed to know more and share more of the rational side of the faith for those who had an intellectual hurdle to overcome.

I can still struggle feeling stupid. I take great comfort in the fact that those who followed Jesus were not educated; they were everyday men and woman (Acts 4:13). The rational aspects of the Christian faith are not complicated and do not require seminary training to understand. They are reasonable, biblical, and accessible. That is why 1 Peter 3:15 says, "But in your hearts set apart Christ as Lord. Always be prepared to give an answer to everyone who asks you to give the reason for the hope that you have. But do this with gentleness and respect."

We must be prepared to share both our experience and our reason. Being prepared is learning and sharing. Sharing our reasons means we have rational aspects to our faith. Most important are the critical, historical, and biblical understanding of the divinity of Jesus and his resurrection.

Wade's Story

My father died when I was two years old, so I never really knew him. My sister died when I was in the fifth grade. Thus, I learned two lessons early in life: (1) life has sorrows and (2) death is inevitable. Somewhere around six years of age, even the Santa Claus myth came to an abrupt end. I cannot speak for others in my age group regarding how they responded, but I clearly remember thinking I had been shafted. Why would adults tell me something they knew was not true?

Around the age of six, the first seeds of my skepticism were probably planted. My father's untimely early death reinforced that skepticism, and my sister's death added fuel. By the time I was eleven or twelve, I was beginning to bump into big questions about life, death, and the purpose of my existence.

Fast forward to my teen years where school, sports, and social-izing made up my day-to-day world. I can recall being thirteen or so and thinking how much time I had till I would be forty-five. I did not see much need to engage the big questions of life although I had clearly identified them by this time. I knew that if there was no ulti-mate answer as to why we were here then there was not much point in doing anything except living in the moment, and at that point in time, I felt like there were a lot of moments to spare.

My mother, like most of my friends' mothers, was a regular churchgoer. That meant I was a regular churchgoer too. We were Methodists. I do not remember many of the sermons, but I do remember that Christ's divinity and the proof of the resurrection were never presented in a manner that caught my attention. Nor do I recall any pulpit conversations about the existence of God or a Christian perspective on suffering and evil.

Generally, my time during these Sundays was spent in a pretty passive mode. However, I liked some of the songs, and I enjoyed getting up to go to communion. One particular communion oppor-tunity we sang a hymn in which God was invoked to cure his chil-dren's warring madness. My friend and I found that line particularly humorous, but the reasoning was lost for the most part on those sitting around us. But I digress.

Around sixteen years of age, I really started what I will call the search. If I was wasting my time in church then I wanted to at least know it was a waste of time. On the other hand, if there was some-thing to be had from all this then I wanted to know what it was and how it could be known.

The Search Begins

I went to see the pastor of my church, and he was quite sur-prised that I was asking the questions I was asking. I simply wanted to know what proof he had of God and if he had any, could he share it with me. I got a book he recommended, and I tried to read it. Looking back, my guess is I was handed a philosophy book from seminary. In any case, I found it unintelligible and concluded that if this was the best proof I could hope for then I was out of luck.

I was now officially jaded. If you wanted to speak to me about how Christ changed your life, I was likely to tell you I had the same experience with bad mayonnaise. To be clear, I had not rejected the possibility of a God, and by extension, a savior; I just wanted more proof than a profession based solely upon what someone felt. I did not trust feelings as a sole source of truth, at least when it came to something so important.

The matter simmered for a number of years, during which I would classify myself as a low-level believer. That is, I concluded the likelihood of a God was better than the likelihood that he did not exist, but I was not satisfied with the insubstantial evidence I had been exposed to.

By then, I was in my twenties, I was married, and I'd been in a number of churches for a number of years. Methodist, nondenominational, Baptist, a short stint at a charismatic church, back to Methodist, and finally back to nondenominational. I was a traveling churchgoer, so I heard a lot of sermons in a lot of venues, but I never heard anything that made me think there was a rational basis for whatever I believed.

Then a biochemistry professor at LSU made an offhand comment one day that made me sit straight up. He was explaining how amino acids are right-handed and left-handed, and that protein synthesis in the body can only take place with left-handed amino acids. This changed nothing in my mind until he said, "And this proves the existence of God."

I did not take his statement as gospel, but it did pique my interest to the point that I began to wonder anew if there was a means to rationally answer life's ultimate questions. It was somewhere around this time that I received my most recent subscription to *Newsweek*. The lead story on the cover had a headline that read something like this: "What Can Science Tell Us about God?"

The Search Quickens

Now the search was really underway. I looked through the quotes in the article and saw that most of them dealt with cosmology, so off I went to some of those sources. Without going into extended detail, it was becoming clear to me that a compelling case could be made independent of the Bible that there is a God. The overwhelming evidence that the universe had a beginning impressed me tremendously. I knew that a universe that was not eternal was also a universe that was created. "Does God exist?" was a question that could actually be answered!

That led me to the Bible and a long search, still continuing, to see if it is an accurate and trustworthy source of information.

I noticed several places in the New Testament that spoke of scriptures that proved Jesus was Messiah. I cannot tell you how many times I read lines like that without grasping their significance. Finally, with some great commentaries and some wonderful external resources, I began to appreciate how the Old Testament prepared the way for the Messiah's place in history as recorded by the New Testament.

For me, a journey that began somewhere around the time when I was six years old was finally completed somewhere around the age of twenty-five. I no longer had to speak only about what I felt; I could also speak confidently about what I knew. Skepticism was replaced by certainty. It is actually possible to know that there is a God, that Jesus is divine, and that the resurrection is a fact.

The Search Shared

I was recently talking to my best friend in high school. As with many friendships forged in high school, we no longer enjoy the frequency of speaking that we once did. He was back in town to bury his mother, and we began to reminisce a bit. In high school, we were very similar in thought and deed, which meant if you wanted to speak to one skeptic you were going to get a double dose.

Shortly after the funeral, we went to dinner before he had to return home. I found out some things I never knew. For example, his father had been an abusive alcoholic and my friend had adopted an avoidance strategy that often entailed spending the weekend at my house. Who knew?

But then he said something startling because the alcoholic father he was describing was not the man I knew. Sometime after we had become friends, his dad was driving to Mississippi with his mother when he pulled off the road. She asked where he was going, and he told her he had to go inside. By inside, he meant inside the church he had just passed. So somewhere in Mississippi, the dad switched from skeptic to believer, and according to the son, he was never the same. Violence was replaced by patience, and his need for alcohol was removed.

It occurred to me while we were talking that his father represented the pure emotional recognition that he was in need of a savior. On the other hand, his son and I both represented a need for a rational basis for our faith. As a side note, my friend noted how his journey to faith has been a slow one, and that he, too, was looking for rational answers. He left with some books in his hands and with conversations yet to be held.[2]

Kevin and my personal stories are nearly polar opposites. My best friend's story and his own father's story are nearly polar opposites. Some have reached a saving faith simply from the emotional confirmation that told them they were changed. Others need to have the facts checked and verified.

Our belief is that many churches rely heavily—perhaps too heavily—upon the "changed life" testimony. Many skeptics will not be swayed by personal statements because, as we have already noted, personal beliefs are personal beliefs and therefore outside the scrutiny of others. Since this is the case, personal beliefs can lack the power to sway others. In other words, many view personal beliefs as lacking any form of objectivity.

The Challenge

We are in an age of skepticism that is saturated in relativistic thinking. "Keep your faith to yourself!" is now an expectation of the

---

[2]   The friend has recently been baptized in his home church.

skeptic, but it gets worse. Today, skeptics are generally convinced that we religious folk are not the brightest of the bright. In fact, we are often viewed with ridicule.

The irony of this type of relativism is there's not much relativity to be found. All things may be relative (actually they cannot, but that is another topic), but from the skeptic's perspective, their view of what is right is often much more correct than the believer's view. Little wonder that many denominations are shrinking and there is now a rising trend of "nones." Pew Research Center estimates that 20 percent of the American public and more than 30 percent of the population that is under thirty years old are now religiously unaffiliated.

However, the trend in "nones" has recently accelerated. Now, approximately one out of six adults in America describe themselves as atheists, and nearly 14 percent report no religious affiliation whatsoever.[3]

That is the bad news. The good news, provided by the same Pew report, indicates that over 65 percent indicate a belief in God, but that may be tempered by nearly 60 percent reporting that they feel connected to nature. Whatever the personal beliefs reported about spirituality, it is clear that these feelings do not translate into religious affiliation or regular church attendance. The vast majority of the "nones" reject organized religion and indicate an overemphasis on rules, politics, money, and power as their primary objections for avoiding church.

Politics? Rules? Money? Power? None of these have a thing to do with the pillars of our faith. If we assume the complaints are well grounded, it means that churches just may be spending too much time on matters that are not really central to the Christian message. On the other hand, if we assume the complaints are excuses to avoid church altogether, then they are simply avoidance strategies. Or to be fair, perhaps they are unfounded assumptions.

If unfounded assumption are the case, then the real value of churches has been lost on those making the complaints. In either

---

[3] "'Nones' on the Rise," Pew Research Center, http://www.pewforum. org/2012/10/09/nones-on-the-rise.

case, it is quite likely the pillars have not been communicated or valued. Neither possibility is a good one.

Make no mistake, there is a pushback against the Christian worldview, and the answer to this rising tide of skepticism must come from two places: the head and the heart. That said, there has always been a pushback against what we believe, even in the days immediately preceding the resurrection. We should not be surprised. After all, the central basis for our faith is that the Son of God rose three days after he was crucified. Nothing to raise skepticism in that claim, right?

Shortly after the resurrection, Peter found himself in Jerusalem, speaking to an audience comprised mostly of very skeptical Jews. According to Acts 3:12–25, a man was healed by Peter and the crowd was abuzz. "Who is this man and where does he get the ability to do what he just did?" were undoubtedly on the tongues of many who had just witnessed the event. Peter answered all their questions and also provided the basis for his actions.

> When Peter saw this, he said to them: "Fellow Israelites, why does this surprise you? Why do you stare at us as if by our own power or godliness we had made this man walk? The God of Abraham, Isaac and Jacob, the God of our fathers, has glorified his servant Jesus. You handed him over to be killed, and you disowned him before Pilate, though he had decided to let him go. You disowned the Holy and Righteous One and asked that a murderer be released to you. You killed the author of life, but God raised him from the dead. We are witnesses of this. By faith in the name of Jesus, this man whom you see and know was made strong. It is Jesus's name and the faith that comes through him that has completely healed him, as you can all see. Now, fellow Israelites, *I know that you acted in ignorance*, as did your leaders. But this is *how God fulfilled what he had fore-*

told through all the prophets, saying that his Messiah would suffer. Repent, then, and turn to God, so that your sins may be wiped out, that times of refreshing may come from the Lord, and that he may send the Messiah, who has been appointed for you—even Jesus. Heaven must receive him until the time comes for God to restore everything, as he promised long ago through his holy prophets. *For Moses said, 'The Lord your God will raise up for you a prophet like me from among your own people; you must listen to everything he tells you.'* Anyone who does not listen to him will be completely cut off from their people. Indeed, beginning with Samuel, all the prophets who have spoken have foretold these days. *And you are heirs of the prophets and of the covenant God made with your fathers.* (Emphasis added)

There was a whole lot happening in these few verses. Peter informed the crowd that he had nothing to do with the healing; it was an act of God. He then used the opportunity and the crowd's bewilderment to get to the points he wanted to make.

First, he noted that Christ was killed in ignorance. This is a very important point that speaks to what a Second Temple Jew anticipated from their Messiah, and we will devote much attention to that in another chapter.[4] Then, he made a statement that sounded very similar indeed to the one Jesus made on resurrection Sunday while walking with the two men to Emmaus, as recorded in Luke 24.

---

[4] Solomon completed the first temple around 950 B.C. It was destroyed in 586 B.C. by Nebuchadnezzar. Zerubbabel, the governor of Judad, rebuilt the temple but to a smaller scale. Around 17 B.C., King Herod began an extensive renovation of the temple and substantial completion occurred around 4 B.C. Renovations and upgrades continued until seven years before the temple was destroyed in 70 A.D. by the Romans. According to 2nd Chronicles, the glory of God dwelt in the first temple but there is no record of God's presence occupying the second temple.

It was a tactful person indeed, who, in a few sentences, could first indict a crowd for their complicity in Christ's death, reminded the crowd that their own scripture described why Christ had to die, and then amazingly concluded by noting that those listening were heirs of the prophets who had foretold the death of Christ. Peter's response to the crowd that day is a model for every Christian to analyze and internalize.

The Head

We believe it is quite likely that Peter was recalling the events of that day and throughout Acts when he wrote his first epistle. Written thirty-five years or so after the resurrection, chapter 3 contains one of the more familiar phrases from the letter.

> But in your hearts revere Christ as Lord. Always be prepared to give an answer to everyone who asks you to give the reason for the hope that you have. But do this with gentleness and respect. (1 Peter 3:15)

Peter's actions in Acts translate into a general course of action that is expected to form the basis for how we speak to the skeptic. We are to be prepared to give an answer for the hope we have, and we are to do so gently and respectfully. Peter certainly followed his own advice in the verses just cited. To remind the audience members they were all heirs to the prophets and to God's covenant immediately after pointing out they had murdered the Messiah was a wonderful example of gentleness, respect, and diplomacy.

But within that gentleness and respect was truth; truth that could be grasped and understood by the audience. Peter was indeed prepared to give a gentle and respectful answer to anyone who heard him on that day thirty or so years before he penned 1 Peter.

We have all been told to be prepared to give a reason for the hope we have. Many people, as we have said, believe this means we tell our story. But we think the scripture is actually calling here for us to be prepared to give a rational basis for our belief. We draw that conclusion because of the scripture that immediately follows. It is just as important to the point Peter is making and should not be left out of any discussion of this nature.

And the Heart

> Keeping a clear conscience, so that those who speak maliciously against your good behavior in Christ may be ashamed of their slander. (1 Peter 3:16)

Now Peter spoke of how we behave because of who we are and taken in total, the message is this: Be prepared to share what you know so that others will recognize how that knowledge, and the transformative nature of that knowledge, are inextricably bound.

As we see, the head and the heart are both in play in Peter's scripture. They should also be in play not only in our lives but in our testimonies. Yet we are not so sure that this is commonly the case for today's Christian. Answering today's skeptic requires rational justification for the existence of God, the divinity of Christ, and the historical nature of the resurrection. But it also requires the evidence of a changed life. These were the expectations of Peter a few years after Christianity was birthed, and they remain the expectations two thousand years later.

What Does This Mean to the Church?

We will develop a recurring theme in the following chapters that the central tenets of the Christian faith are beyond the realm of the average church attendee to articulate well. If our conclusion is correct, we should not be surprised at reports similar to the Pew research we cited that shows church growth is shrinking along with the number of people who report frequent church attendance.

You cannot sustain what you cannot substantiate, and Christianity is no exception. Said another way, we cannot speak persuasively about Jesus as the way, the truth, and the life if we cannot affirm that God is real, Jesus is divine, the resurrection occurred, and suffering and evil are not a death blow to an all-loving God.

Contrast the apparent inability of the typical Christian of today to always give an account of why we believe with the Christians of the early church. Following the model of Jesus, Peter, and Paul, they fueled the church's explosive growth by proving insistently that Christ's claims were validated years earlier by Moses and the prophets. Add a resurrection that produced multiple sightings post-tomb, and every Christian of that day had all the evidence needed to proclaim the good news. The early church knew how to communicate these truths, and the mission of every church today is to produce believers who can do the same.

So far, we have begun an argument for a return to the historical origins for the spread of the gospel message, and we have argued that useful defenses for the pillars of Christianity are absolutely essential to the future of Christianity. We are also arguing that useful defenses for the foundations of Christianity are often beyond the scope of the believer to articulate with any degree of confidence. This needs to change if the church is to realize its potential as the hands and feet of Christ.

So we turn our attention now to the first pillar of Christianity. How do we know the God of the Bible exists? As important as that answer is, it is even more important to know how we can explain that position to a skeptic. Chapter 2 begins the journey.

Further Reflection

Central theme: You cannot sustain what you cannot substantiate, and Christianity is no exception. Said another way, we cannot speak persuasively about Jesus as the way, the truth, and the life if we cannot affirm God is real, Jesus is divine, the resurrection occurred, and suffering and evil are not a death blow to an all-loving God.

Reflective Activities

1. List at least three arguments a skeptic is likely to use to challenge Christianity.
2. What are the biggest doubts you encounter about your own faith? Or, said another way, what topics that challenge Christianity cause you the most concern?
3. Is J. Robert Machen on to something in the introduction of this book? Do his points resonate today?

Chapter 2

The Big Picture
Why Is There Anything at All?

As long as the universe had a beginning, we would suppose it had a creator.[1]

It is said that an argument is what convinces reasonable men and a proof is what it takes to convince even an unreasonable man. With the proof now in place, cosmologists can no longer hide behind the possibility of a past-eternal universe. There is no escape: They have to face the problem of a cosmic beginning.[2]

Many Christians recoil from science, believing that it is a threat to their faith. We hope that this chapter proves otherwise. We have compiled a series of quotes from different scientists and philosophers, and we have included them to help the reader better understand that science has not buried God. In fact, as you will see, that is not the case at all.

---

[1] Stephen Hawking, *A Brief History of Time* [New York: Bantam Books, 1988], 140
[2] Alexander Vilenkin, *Many Worlds in One: The Search for Other Universes* [New York: Hill & Wang, 2006], 176)

We spend the majority of our time in this chapter focused on conversations about the origins of the universe, and we do that for the following simple reason. If the universe has been purposefully created, then we have taken the first big step toward determining whether the God of the Bible is that Creator.

We did not spend much time on evolution beyond one short paragraph, and you will see why that is the case when you reach the quote by C. S. Lewis. The arguments about evolution are, if you will, in chapter 22 in the book of the universe. We are much more interested in chapter 1 because chapter 1 explains "in the beginning." So, with that background, let's begin with the big questions that demand big answers.

Ultimate Questions, Ultimate Answers?

How did we get here? Can we know that God exists, or are we left to believe what cannot be verified? How do we answer skeptics who wonder why we are so misguided as to think this universe was created, Jesus was God, and he rose from the dead? The claims do indeed seem to go from wild to unbelievably out of control. At least that is what the world assumes. But we know differently, don't we?

Or do we? Clearly the world ain't buying what we are selling, which begs this question: Just what exactly are we selling? It is common in Europe to see churches poorly attended and to note a general apathy in church worship. Why mess with something you do not think is useful? America is different though. Right? America still demonstrates a "one nation under God" mentality, where the vast majority of the country accepts God as a reality and the Bible as truth. Right? Right?

Recognizing an Important Shift

Recently, a conversation was had with a pastor. He came from a biker background, and he had spent much time among some of the more infamous motorcycle gangs trying to spread the gospel. He had been told time and time again by bikers that they knew there is a God but they are just not interested in bowing their knee to him. Historically, in our culture, the next generation had been prepared by the current generation with a worldview that includes God. Accordingly, the church operated from that same framework, and we could dispense with proofs of the tenets of our faith because they were generally not needed. Or so we thought.

But this same pastor noted that the willingness to acknowledge God as a given has shifted radically in a very short time. The assumption that a skeptic has even a rudimentary knowledge of church is not justified anymore, much less that there is an intrinsic reality that there is a God. Today we see many states that have a clear majority of citizens who attend church rarely or never. We have a culture that grows not just intolerant of the Christian worldview but is derisive of the lowbrows who believe in Spaghetti Monsters in the sky. There is now a rising trend of "apatheists"—folks who do not even attempt to search for answers to the four basic pillars the Christian Church must defend. To these people, we are not merely wrong, we are entirely irrelevant.

Pockets of churches are beginning to recognize the necessity of sharpening their apologetic skills so that they may be prepared to give a clear account of what they believe. Institutions such as Biola University and apologists such as Ravi Zacharias, William Lane Craig, Hugh Ross, John Lennox, and Fritz Schaefer are working tirelessly to present the case for our cause along with many others as well. Likewise, churches are starting apologetics teams and hosting seminars.

All good! Still, the effort is too small, and we fear the urgency is not realized in many churches as they continue to operate with outmoded assumptions and strategies. The intent is honorable, but the results are often less than desired.

There are several advantages to having firm, rational convictions about the Christian pillars. You will be able to speak to a skeptic in such a way that allows them to challenge what you believe, rather than you challenging what they believe. This is no small point. Telling a person why they are wrong can and often does lead to a defensive person. Telling a person why they are wrong without being able to articulate the basis for that evaluation can create fireworks.

Asking a person to critique your own viewpoint, however, is far less combative and offers many obvious advantages. If the person is hostile to your position, they may well attack it with gusto. Fine. Iron sharpens iron, and each time the person attacks you, your own faith defenses will be sharpened. Also, it is very powerful for a skeptic to witness attacks that are met with love and compassion.

Stated simply, *we are not trying to win arguments. We are attempting to persuade people to accept Christ based on their own conclusions.* None of us should be interested in proving our intellectual shrewdness, nor should we celebrate crushing a skeptic. If we engage skeptics with a real effort to befriend them and because we genuinely like and respect them, then we have an opportunity to ask them to challenge us, and we can remove the charged atmosphere that makes so many of us afraid to share our faith.

Reacting to an Increasingly Skeptical Worldview

We live in an age of skepticism and, as we said, if we start with your story or my story it may be dismissed as a result of delirium. And, if your story is the best you can do then it sounds very familiar to the relativistic drumbeat that has been pounding in a lot of skeptics' heads for years. "Alas, that might be true for you, but it is certainly not true for me." That is a mild form of skepticism. A more severe form might attack you as unsophisticated, your thinking as childish, and your beliefs dangerous and in need of eradication. This response might be something you would expect from someone identifying themselves as a new atheist.[3]

Having appropriate answers to challenges for the Christian pillars is absolutely essential if we are to engage the culture that now exists and is rapidly growing. We used to say it was important to train our children going off to college so they would not have their faith mortally wounded. That is still true today, but we would be beyond naive if we do not recognize that the attacks are no longer limited to

---

[3] Daniel Dennett, Richard Dawkins, Christopher Hitchens, and Sam Harris have been coined the "new atheists." Much of their popular writings center on the refutation of theism and the removal of all religion from the public square.

vitriolic professors on college campuses. Today, the attacks are virtually omnipresent from nearly every facet of our culture. The church has no option; it must rise to this challenge or continue to lose the intellectual high ground it possesses even as it defends it weakly, if at all.

Christ himself said that the gates of hell will not prevail against his church. We believe Christ knew what he was talking about. We also know that the church is the hands and feet, soldiers on the ground, for the cause of Christ. It should not be lost on any of us that the first apologetic for Christ's divinity was issued by Christ himself, on the road to Emmaus. As we will see in future chapters, the apostles quickly understood how to frame arguments for the people of their time so as to allow those people to criticize the facts as they were presented. We must do the same.

One thing has definitely changed since John the Revelator penned his final "Come Quickly, Lord Jesus," and that is our understanding of the physical world. Science has brought tremendous progress to civilization, and many believe that science has placed God in a box that is continually shrinking or perhaps is already infinitely small.

Neil deGrasse Tyson sums up this view of science very well:

> If you don't understand something and the community of physicists don't understand it, that means God did it? Is that how you want to play this game? Is that how you want to invoke your evidence for God, then God is an ever-receding pocket of scientific ignorance that's getting smaller and smaller and smaller as time moves on.[4]

Whew. How would you answer this criticism? This is a top-down, presumptive argument that assumes the inferiority of the

---

[4] "The Moon, the Tides, and Why Neil deGrasse Tyson is Colbert's God," January 20, 2011, The Science Network, video.

Christian worldview. In fact, it dangles that presumption in front of the Christian with a disdainful expectation that nothing can be said to the contrary.

Neil deGrasse Tyson is wrong. As we shall document, there is compelling evidence for God, for Christ's divinity, for the resurrection, and for an appropriate understanding of suffering and sovereignty. Since Tyson starts with science, we will do so as well. George F. Will helps us set the stage.

Chaos or Purpose?

George F. Will is a well-known columnist. He writes mostly about politics and occasionally about baseball. In one of his columns, however, he wrote about neither. In the article "Finding Our Place in the Universe," Will spoke of a new telescope that will extend the work of the Hubble Telescope and advance knowledge about what he called a "stupendous improbability." Here were his words: "How did material complexity, then single-cell life, then animals and consciousness emerge from *chaos*?" (emphasis ours).

Will continued. "Webb (the new telescope) will not shed light on two interesting questions: How many universes are there? Is everything the result of a meaningless *cosmic sneeze* or of an intentional *First Cause*?"

Will's job is to provide a succinct, one-thousand-word column on a regular basis, and these columns are expected to elicit reflective responses from his readers. If that is the case, George left his readers with a real barn burner this time.

"Is everything the result of a meaningless cosmic sneeze or of an intentional First Cause?" is the question for the ages. Is it answerable, or is it an unsolvable enigma? Notice also that Will was well aware of the implications of the question. First Cause, capitalized, signifies the need for a Creator, while a cosmic sneeze suggests quite the opposite.

So far, so good. Where Will deviated from his usual high standard of logical dissection of information was when he opined: "How did material complexity, then single-cell life, then animals and consciousness emerge from chaos?"

We think Will has gone a bridge too far; who said chaos is the instigator of the order we see in our universe? If there is a First Cause, then there is nothing chaotic about the beginning of the universe and its ultimate support of our tiny little blue planet, and we are here for a reason. If, on the other hand, there is no evidence to support a First Cause, then it is entirely rational to speak of a cosmic sneeze and his ruminations about consciousness emerging from chaos could then be a subject worthy of *Final Jeopardy*.

Unpacking the Problem: How Did the Universe Get Here?

R. C. Sproul in *Not a Chance* identified four possible explanations for the universe's existence. These options embrace all logical possibilities, and therefore one of them is the ultimate explanation for the universe.[5]

The universe is an illusion. It does not exist.

1. The universe has no beginning and is uncaused. This is Will's cosmic sneeze.
2. The universe is self-created.
3. The universe is caused by something that is eternal.

Option 1: The Universe Is an Illusion

Perhaps we are not real. Maybe we are nothing more than brains in a jar, and the perceived reality that surrounds us is nothing more than a product of neural pathways. Then again, maybe not.

There is an old blues song, "Shout Bamalama," recorded by the late great Otis Redding. Words to the tune go something like this:

> Preacher and a deacon out walkin' one day;
> Out come a bear along the way;
> Preacher told the deacon to say a prayer;
> He said, ain't no prayer gonna kill that bear we
> got to run for it!

---

5   R. C. Sproul, *Not a Chance: The Myth of Chance in Modern Science and Cosmology* (Grand Rapids: Baker Books, 1994)

We are not aware of Otis's theological training, but we do think his conclusion is appropriate. If this world were not real, then these arguments do not matter. There is no bear, there is no pain, there is no joy, and everything is an illusion. Understandably, this option does not receive much attention, and we have already given it more than it probably deserves.

Option 2: The Universe Is Eternal and Has Always Existed

This option is where contemporary science used to rest. Now, it is hard to find anyone arguing for an uncaused, eternal universe. We will explain why this is so when we get to the last option.

Option 3: The Universe Is Self-Created

The universe is self-created. Stop and think about this one for a moment, for it basically says you can get something from nothing. Although everything we know and experience tells us this is illogical, we will see in a moment why more and more emphasis is being placed on this option as the best explanation for the universe's existence by some cosmologists. When self-creation is floated as plausible it should give some insight to the actual probabilities of an uncaused universe.

Option 4: The Universe Is Created by an Eternal, Uncaused First Cause

Note that option 2 and option 4 both agree that something must be eternal. In option 2, the universe is uncaused and simply *is*. In option 4, the universe is caused by something that is uncaused and simply *is*.

Recognizing the eternal nature of something removes one of the first arguments raised about the possibility that option 4 is correct. "Who created God?" is not a fatal question. In fact, it is not even a major impediment. Something must be eternal. That something might be the universe or its proposed father, the multiverse, or that something could just as logically be the First Cause. The only way to know is to investigate the evidence, and that is what we will now do.

Evidence for a Creator?

Arno Penzias was part of a research team that discovered the background radiation from the big bang. Those two words tend to evoke trepidation in some people of faith because they are supposedly incongruent with God as Creator. Maybe not. Here is what Penzias said about the big bang in *Cosmos, Bios, Theos.*[6]

> In order to achieve consistency with our observations we must, according to Einstein's Theory of General Relativity, assume not only creation of matter and energy out of nothing, but creation of space and time as well. Moreover, this creation must be very delicately balanced. The amount of energy given to the emerging matter must be enough to move it fast enough to escape the bonds of gravity, but not so fast that the particles lose all contact with each other. Enough of the initially created matter must pull together under gravity to form galaxies, stars, and planetary systems which allow for life. Thus the second "improbable" property of the early universe, almost as improbable as creation out of nothing, is an exquisitely delicate balance between matter and energy. Third—and this one puzzles scientists at least as much as the first two—somehow all these pieces, each without having any proper contact with the others, without having any way of communication, all must have appeared with the same balance between matter and energy at the same instant.

---

[6]   Henry Margenau and Roy Abraham Varghese, ed., *Cosmos, Bios, Theos: Scientists Reflect on Science, God, and the Origins of the Universe, Life, and Homo Sapiens* (Peru, Illinois: Open Court Publishing, 1992), 82

According to Einstein's general relativity, we must assume the creation of space, time, matter, and energy from nothing. Also, there must be an incredible balance of matter and energy so that the universe had time to do all the things necessary for life on our tiny little planet. And finally, there had to be some means of communication (physical laws) either created simultaneously or prior to the creation of space, time, matter, and energy from nothing.

Henry Margenau, professor emeritus in physics from Yale University, said this from the same book:

> Referring to physical laws... They surely could not have developed by chance or accident. What, then, is the answer to the question concerning the origin of the innumerable laws of nature? I know only one answer that is adequate to their universal validity: They were created by God.[7]

Our intent is not to go into an exhaustive apologetic for the existence of the universe. There are a number of resources available for further reading if there is a deeper interest. That said, we do want to extend this conversation a little further to show why a universe created by an eternal First Cause is the most logical explanation for the universe's existence.

Three very important observations can be had from Penzias's quote:

1. The universe began to exist.
2. The universe is delicately balanced to ultimately provide a suitable habitat on our earth.
3. The universe is guided by an information system that precedes or coexists with its creation.

Recently deceased, Stephen Hawking is one of the greatest minds in the sum total of human existence. Hawking wrote a book

---

[7] Ibid., 61.

a few years ago entitled *A Brief History of Time*.[8] In this widely popular book, Hawking took due notice of the complexity of the universe and the implications that the initial conditions were very finely tuned, and the evidence does indeed seem to point to a First Cause. Then he dropped this bombshell:

> So long as the universe had a beginning, we would suppose it had a creator (the cosmological argument). But if the universe is really completely self-contained, having no boundary or edge, it would have neither beginning nor end: it would simply be. What place then for a creator?[9]

"So long as the universe had a beginning, we would suppose it had a creator." Hawking's words. But he was not content to stop there, and he then posits a boundless universe; a universe where time is eternal and the universe therefore is eternal as well (option 2). What place then for a Creator?

Is Hawking on to something? Has he discovered a dodge to a created universe? The short answer is no.

Henry "Fritz" Schaefer is no intellectual slouch himself. A professor of quantum chemistry at the University of Georgia, Schaefer is one of the most cited chemists in the world for his professional work. Fritz had this to say about Hawking's musings in his book *Science and Christianity: Conflict or Coherence?*[10]

> Hawking and Hartle's no boundary proposal begins by adopting a grossly oversimplified model of the universe. Then the authors make time imaginary, and prove in their terribly restricted model that the universe has neither beginning nor end. The flaw in the exercise is that the authors never

---

8   Stephen Hawking, *A Brief History of Time* (New York: Bantam Books, 1988)
9   Ibid., 141.
10 *Schaefer, Henry F. Science and Christianity: Conflict or Coherence?* Watkinsville, GA: Apollos Trust, 2013.

go back to real time. Thus the notion that the universe has neither beginning nor end is something that exists in mathematical terms only. In real time, to which we as human beings are necessarily attached, rather than in Hawking's use of imaginary time, there will always be a singularity, that is, a beginning of time.[11]

Perhaps Schaefer had misread Hawking or distorted Hawking's words. That was not the case as can be seen in his words:

> In an obviously contradictory statement in *A Brief History of Time*, Hawking actually concedes this point. What we are seeing in this situation is Hawking versus Hawking. I view the following statement as Hawking speaking in his right mind: "When one goes back to the real time in which we live, however, there will still appear to be singularities... In real time, the universe has a beginning and an end at singularities that form a boundary to space-time and at which the laws of science break down."[12]
>
> In real time, the universe has a beginning and an end.[13]
>
> As long as the universe had a beginning, we would suppose it had a creator.[14]

As we said, Hawking is brilliant. In *A Brief History of Time*, he took his best shot at an eternal universe but was not able to finalize the effort. So where does Hawking go? Interestingly, he wrote another book entitled *The Grand Design* and made this assertion:

---

[11] Ibid., 64–65.
[12] Ibid., 65.
[13] Stephen Hawking, *A Brief History of Time* (New York: Bantam Books, 1988)
[14] Ibid.

> Because there is a law such as gravity, the universe
> can and will create itself from nothing.[15]

One thing to notice is that Hawking left behind option two and now embraces option three, a self-created universe. Why? Simply put, the evidence for option two is not compelling. A close examination of Hawking's latest assertion leads to the same conviction.

We now turn to John Lennox for an examination and critique of Hawking's self-created universe. Lennox, like Schaefer, is no small academic force. A professor of mathematics at Oxford, Lennox spends a great deal of time critiquing claims such as those made by Hawking from a Christian perspective. In fact, Lennox went through the effort to write a rebuttal to *The Grand Design* entitled *God and Stephen Hawking: Whose Design Is It Anyway?*[16] Here is a brief excerpt from Lennox on Hawking's proposal.

> Suppose, to make matters clearer, we replace the
> universe by a jet engine and then are asked to
> explain it. Shall we account for it by mention-
> ing the personal agency of its inventor, Sir Frank
> Whittle? Or shall we follow Hawking: dismiss
> personal agency and explain the jet engine by say-
> ing that it arose naturally from a physical law?[17]

Lennox correctly pointed out that Hawking had confused a law with agency. The agent or cause, if you will, implements the law; laws do not create agents. For the sake of argument though, we will concede Hawking's assertion that the universe will create itself from nothing because there is a law of gravity.

---

[15] Stephen Hawking and Leonard Mlodinow, *The Grand Design* (New York: Bantam Books, 2010), 180

[16] Lennox, John C. *God and Stephen Hawking: Whose Design Is It Anyway?* Oxford: Lion, 2011.

[17] Ibid., 36.

$$F_g = G \frac{m_1 m_2}{r^2}$$

Here we see the law of gravity, and in simple language, it says that any two objects will attract based upon their mass, the distance between them, and a gravitational constant. Now one can correctly wonder why there would be a law that governs gravitational attraction if there were no such thing as objects with mass or even such a thing as space that would create distances between these objects. Why would a law exist to govern things that do not exist? We agree with Margenau's view that physical laws must have a cause. And we agree with his conclusion that God is that cause.

This is a good time to point out the miracle of creation. We turn to George Smoot to provide the details. Smoot received the Nobel Prize in physics in 2006 for his work on the Cosmic Background Explorer (COBE), a research project that documented expected "wrinkles" in the space-time fabric as a result of the big bang. Smoot wrote a book entitled, appropriately enough, *Wrinkles in Time: The Greatest Discovery of the Century*,[18] in which he explains what happened just after the big bang.

> At a ten-millionth of a trillionth of a trillionth of a trillionth of a second after the big bang—the earliest moment about which we can sensibly talk, and then only with some suspension of disbelief—all the universe we can observe today was the tiniest fraction of the size of a proton. Space and time had only just begun. (Remember, the universe did not expand into existing space after the big bang, its expansion created space-time as it went.)[19]

---

[18] Smoot, George. *Wrinkles in Time: The Greatest Discovery of the Century*. New York: Morrow, 1993.

[19] Ibid., 283.

Space and time had only just begun? The entire universe the fraction of the size of a proton? Smoot deduced that since space and time had just begun, all the matter in the universe appeared at a single instant. Then, this matter expanded, creating the very space that this matter expands into. Ultimately, these conditions provided incredibly balanced conditions that allowed for star formation, galaxies, solar systems, planets, and eventually our planet, with its ability to support life.

This is the "stupendous improbability" that Will alluded to when we began this chapter. We believe creation miracle is a better explanation than stupendous improbability. The odds of creating a universe such as ours are infinitesimally small when viewed as a product of chance. To dodge creation, we are left with one other possibility.

The Multiverse?

Martin Rees is a proponent of the multiverse. In *Just Six Numbers: The Deep Forces that Shape the Universe*,[20] he provided his explanation for why the multiverse is necessary. Here is a recap:

1. A universe like ours is exceedingly improbable.
2. We know God doesn't exist.
3. Therefore, there must be an infinite number of universes.
4. We hit the jackpot with our universe.

Rees understood the problem of explaining our universe when he said our universe is exceedingly improbable. Maybe there are an infinite number of universes, and if we have that many, we should not be surprised that one of them got it "right" for life to exist and for us to be wondering about matters such as these.

Although Rees is quite sure God does not exist, it is important to note that he provided no evidence to dispel that possibility. Remember what Hawking said: "As long as the universe had a begin-

---

[20] Rees, Martin. *Just Six Numbers: The Deep Forces That Shape the Universe.* New York: Member of the Perseus Books Group, 2000.

ning, we could suppose it had a creator." Rees dodged that conclusion by saying there are an infinite number of universes.

But his dodge has problems, not the least of which is the introduction of a problem even more bewildering than what we have. If it is so difficult to explain a single universe, how to account for the complexity that would be necessary to create an infinite number of universes?

Regardless of how many universes one posits, it seems necessary to constrain the creation of multiple universes with the same four possibilities that might explain our single universe. That is, just as the universe might be an illusion, or eternal, or self-created, or created by God, so too for the multiverse. And if the evidence is compelling that our universe has a Creator, then it seems impossible to ignore the implications for this multiverse as well.

The multiverse is being increasingly positioned as a means to avoid creation. Well, as we noted above, there are philosophical limitations to how far you can stretch that argument. We acknowledge that we cannot verify other universes. But as we have noted, that does not preclude us from an explanation of our universe, and as we have seen, there is ample information that supports the need for a Creator to explain its existence.

There will undoubtedly continue to be efforts to bypass a Creator as a necessity to explain our universe. Not only will they confront the facts we have discussed, they will also run up against this final piece of evidence.

In 2012, Hawking had a birthday party. It was a bash where some of the world's foremost physicists were invited to give their papers on the state of cosmology. One gentleman, Alexander Vilenkin, was one of those invited to speak. Vilenkin's paper was entitled *Why Physicists Can't Avoid a Creation Event.* Lisa Grossman reported on the paper's presentation in the magazine *New Science* and wrote these words:

> From the paper, Vilenkin concludes, "All the evidence we have says that the universe has a beginning."[21]

The universe, our universe, has a beginning; this conclusion was derived from a paper delivered at Hawking's seventieth birthday bash. Even if there are an infinite number of universes (and we will likely never know that), our particular universe has a beginning.

Stephen Hawking, one of the most brilliant minds to grace the planet, spent the majority of his academic life looking for explanations for the universe that need not invoke a Creator. He used imaginary time to build a model in which the universe has no beginning and it was found lacking. He theorized a self-created universe that appears out of nothing because of the law of gravity, but that theory is also fatally flawed. He held a birthday party, and at that party, a paper was given that explains why a creation event is unavoidable for our universe.

We now return to Rees's argument one more time to clear up a leap of illogic. Rees said there are an infinite number of universes. We do not know that is true, but we will give him that statement.

However, if there are an infinite number of universes then it is logical that there are an infinite number of possibilities for those universes. If that is the case, it also stands to reason that at least one option would contain an omnipotent, omnipresent God. And, if God is omnipresent, he must be present in every universe (otherwise, he isn't omnipresent). What's sauce for the goose is also sauce for the gander.

George Will's comments helped open this chapter. He asked how the order that we see around us could originate out of chaos. We humbly submit that it cannot. Ravi Zacharias made that point very clear in his book *The End of Reason: A Response to the New Atheists.*[22]

---

[21] Grossman, Lisa. "Why Physicists Can't Avoid a Creation Event." *New Science.* https://www.newscientist.com/article/mg21328474.400-why-physicists-cant-avoid-a-creation-event

[22] Zacharias, Ravi K. *The End of Reason: A Response to the New Atheists.* Grand Rapids, MI: Zondervan, 2008.

I want to add that our arguments for the existence of God do not hinge on the debunking of evolution. Evolution is a straw man that has been thrown up, as if all that needs to be done to achieve the crashing down of belief in God is to posit evolution. Serious intellectuals ought to know that no world view is established on one knockout argument.... For now, all I want to assert is that the atheistic starting point brings us to a contradiction in terms at worst and a random universe at best. In Miracles, C. S. Lewis takes this kind of thinking to task: "Reason might conceivably be found to depend on [another reason] and so on; it would not matter how far this process was carried provided you found Reason coming from Reason at each stage. It is only when you are asked to believe Reason coming from non-reason that you must cry Halt."[23]

Note Zacharias's points carefully. He recognized correctly that a created universe requires a Creator or, to use Lewis's term, Reason. Non-reason, a.k.a. chaos, is not, if you will forgive the redundancy, a reasonable explanation for reason.

A Review of the Options and a Conclusion Based on the Evidence

We return then to our options for the universe.

1. The universe is an illusion. (No.)
2. The universe is eternal. (No.)
3. The universe created itself. (No.)
4. The universe is created by an eternal First Cause. (We believe the evidence is clear.)

---

[23] Ibid., 37.

The current state of science can be summarized succinctly by an observation made nearly thirty-five years ago. The writer is Robert Jastrow, and he was by no means sympathetic to a Creator. That said, note what he said in *God and the Astronomers: New and Expanded Edition*[24] and then recognize his conclusion has only been cemented by the science of subsequent years.

> For the scientist who has lived by his faith in the power of reason, the story ends like a bad dream. He has scaled the mountains of ignorance; he is about to conquer the highest peak; as he pulls himself over the final rock, he is greeted by a band of theologians who have been sitting there for centuries.[25]

More recently, a book was published by Antony Flew. The name may not be familiar to you, but it should be. Antony Flew published a book in 2007 entitled *There Is a God: How the World's Most Notorious Atheist Changed His Mind.*[26] Flew was to the atheist movement what Billy Graham might be to the Christian world.

Recently deceased, Flew had quite a remarkable academic pedigree, including debating C. S. Lewis. His 1950 essay "Theology and Falsification" became the most reprinted philosophical publication of the last half of the twentieth century.

Flew was and still is a formidable force in academia. The contents of *There Is a God* are revealing because they lay bare Flew's long journey from atheism. Flew divided his book into two sections. Part one recounted his denial of the divine; part two took us on his journey to the discovery of the divine. Following are the chapter names for part two, and they should now sound familiar themes to much of what we have said.

---

[24] Jastrow, Robert. *God and the Astronomers: New and Expanded Edition.* New York: W.W. Norton, 1978.

[25] Ibid., 116.

[26] Flew, Antony, and Roy Abraham. Varghese. *There Is a God: How the World's Most Notorious Atheist Changed His Mind.* New York: HarperOne, 2008.

- Chapter 4: A Pilgrimage of Reason
- Chapter 5: Who Wrote the Laws of Nature?
- Chapter 6: Did the Universe Know We Were Coming?
- Chapter 7: How Did Life Go Live?
- Chapter 8: Did Something Come from Nothing?

In his book, Flew provided a quote from Alvin Plantinga, one of the foremost Christian philosophers of our time. Plantinga said: "It speaks very well of Professor Flew's honesty. After all these years of opposing the idea of a Creator, he reverses his position on the basis of the evidence."[27]

Evidence. As noted, we have not tried to exhaust the evidence in this chapter, but we have tried to demonstrate that there is an abundance of it. When skeptics such as Tyson rail that science is placing God in a smaller and smaller and smaller box, the believer can confidently recall the major points of this chapter. Science does not deny God because it was God who created science.

Laying the Groundwork

We have just laid out our argument for a caused universe, and we agree with Hawking that as long as the universe has a beginning, we would presume it has a Creator. That said, the Creator of the universe may or may not be the God of the Bible. That means that the Bible can *possibly* be true since the Bible is a book about God.

Okay, but that doesn't mean the Bible is true. There could be another God outside the God of the Bible. But it is also possible that the God of the Bible is the First Cause that George Will wrote about. One straightforward means of determining the identity of the First Cause is to investigate the claims for Christ's divinity. If Christ is divine, that means he is God incarnate on earth. That will also mean that the God of the Bible is also the God of the universe. With that in mind, our journey now takes us to the question of the divinity of Christ. But first, we take one brief detour on what is often a very bumpy road.

---

[27] Ibid., 72.

Age of the Earth?

Before we move on, we have one last bridge to cross. Many believe the Bible requires an interpretation that leads to a six-thousand-year-old planet. This view is held rather strongly by some camps. On the other hand, many believe the Bible is divinely inspired, and Genesis does not presuppose nor require a six-thousand-year-old earth.

These may be internal conversations, but they have little to do with our four critical areas: (1) the existence of God, (2) the divinity of Christ, (3) the resurrection, and (4) a Christian perspective on pain and suffering. Worship-style, elder-led church governance, women in the pulpit, salvation assured, time of Christ's return—these are just a few areas in which there has been internal disagreement.

Where we should be absolutely unanimous is that God exists, he sent his son as a divine intervener for mankind, and Jesus and Jesus alone is the path to eternal life with the Father.

Interestingly, the early church had its own disagreements about the age of the earth, and we believe it accurate to report that these conversations were about interpretation rather than orthodoxy. To the early church fathers *creatio ex nihilo,* that is, creation of everything from nothing, was orthodoxy. The age of the earth on the other hand was subject to interpretation.

The age of the earth has no impact—none—on the divinity of Christ or the resurrection. As we noted, neither do styles of worship, governance of church, eschatology, or infant baptism. While these topics often produce contentious divisions in the church, none of them contribute or detract from the truth of our faith.

We say this with humility but also with certainty: The church would be better served, and Christ would be better honored, if we spent more time speaking to the world about the hope we have rather than arguing among ourselves about the nuances of our faith.

Conclusion

We have taken a quick journey through the possibilities that might account for why we are here, and we have discovered that the evidence is compelling for a created universe. Consequently, that means the evidence is compelling for a Creator. Is this the God of the Bible? Maybe, maybe not. But if the Creator is the God of the Bible, we would expect that evidence to be found within the pages of the most published book in human history.

How might the Bible tell us that the God of the Bible is the God of the universe? Chapter 3 begins that journey as we investigate whether Jesus was, in fact, divine.

Further Reflection

Central theme: If the universe has been purposefully created, then we have taken the first big step toward determining whether the God of the Bible is that Creator.

Reflective Activities

1. Think about the four possible explanations for the universe posed in your reading:
   a) It is an illusion.
   b) It created itself.
   c) It has always existed and is therefore eternal.
   d) It was created by something that is eternal.
   Are there any other options? What do options c and d have in common?
2. Why not just start with "In the beginning?"
3. How did Hawking frame the cosmological argument in terms of a Creator?
4. Hawking argued for a universe where time has no beginning in *A Brief History of Time* but abandoned that position in his latest book *The Grand Design*. In that book, Hawking argued for a self-created universe. Why?
5. What are some serious flaws in Hawking's latest proposal?
6. Why did we avoid arguments about age of the earth and evolution?

Chapter 3

Is Jesus Divine?

A man who was merely a man and said the sort of things Jesus said would not be a great moral teacher. He would be either a lunatic, on a level with the man who says he is a poached egg, or else he would be the Devil of Hell. You must make your choice. Either this man was, and is, the Son of God; or else he was a madman...or something worse. You can shut Him up for a fool, you can spit at Him and kill him as a demon; or you can fall at His feet and call Him Lord and God. But let us not come with any patronizing nonsense about His being a great human teacher. He has not left that open to us. He did not intend to.[1]

In this chapter, we will make a case for the divine messiahship of Jesus. We will draw upon what others thought of Jesus, what Jesus thought of himself, and what the Jewish culture of that day expected from a Messiah. In the next chapter we will also examine how his closest allies' views changed so dramatically over the course of a weekend.

---

[1] Lewis, C.S. *Mere Christianity*. New York: Harper Collins, 1952, 55–56.

When you have completed these chapters, we trust you will have a deepened awareness of the case for Christ's divinity, as well as information that can be shared with anyone who questions this claim.

If Jesus Christ is God in the flesh, we should see clear evidence that he and he alone can claim divinity. If we see that, then we have credible reason to understand that the Creator of the universe and God the Father are one and the same. Jesus continually refers to God as Father, and he also claimed that he and the Father are one.

We know what Jesus believed, but it is entirely possible that Jesus was wrong, misguided, or perhaps deluded. So how might we go about testing Jesus's claims for divinity? One way is to look at how Jesus defended his divinity postresurrection (we look at evidence for the resurrection in the next chapter). In Luke 24, Jesus provides the first known apologetic when he spoke to Cleopas and his pal on the road to Emmaus. The story is one of the most tongue-in-cheek in scripture: the Son of God inquiring about the Son of God. We pick up Luke 24 for the details.

> Now that same day two of them were going to a village called Emmaus, about seven miles from Jerusalem. They were talking with each other about everything that had happened. As they talked and discussed these things with each other, Jesus himself came up and walked along with them; but they were kept from recognizing him.
>
> He asked them, "What are you discussing together as you walk along?"
>
> They stood still, their faces downcast. One of them, named Cleopas, asked him, "Are you the only one visiting Jerusalem who does not know the things that have happened there in these days?"
>
> "What things?" he asked.
>
> "About Jesus of Nazareth," they replied. "He was a prophet, powerful in word and deed before

God and all the people. The chief priests and our rulers handed him over to be sentenced to death, and they crucified him; but we had hoped that he was the one who was going to redeem Israel. And what is more, it is the third day since all this took place. In addition, some of our women amazed us. They went to the tomb early this morning but didn't find his body. They came and told us that they had seen a vision of angels, who said he was alive. Then some of our companions went to the tomb and found it just as the women had said, but they did not see Jesus."

He said to them, *"How foolish you are, and how slow to believe all that the prophets have spoken! Did not the Messiah have to suffer these things and then enter his glory?"* And beginning with Moses and all the Prophets, he explained to them what was said in all the Scriptures concerning himself. (Luke 24:13–25; emphasis added)

Just What Is a Messiah, Anyway?

We benefit from hindsight, but we can also be hindered by it. It is an easy mistake to read about Jesus and forget that scripture is describing events that, at the time, were often very confusing to those who were actually there.

For example, Jesus's followers never got a firm grasp on the fact that he would suffer and die as an intentional act of atonement before the resurrection. Likewise, the expectations regarding the promised Messiah from the Jewish community at large were quite different from what they saw in Jesus's last week. Again, it was only after the resurrection when the Christian converts connected the dots and understood that Jesus was both Lord and Messiah.

The Messiah was viewed by the Jews as an anointed or appointed man of God, a king from the royal line of David (e.g., Psalm 2:6; Jeremiah 23:5–6). This man, when he came, was expected to be a deliverer for Israel, a man who would rid Israel of her all too common occupations and threats from pagan nations. In addition, he would rebuild or restore the temple to its original specifications and institute true justice with authority given directly from God. It is important to note that none of these tasks carry an expectation of death and later resurrection. To incorrectly suppose that the resurrection was not a total surprise to friend and foe alike lessens the appreciation for the actual events that led to Christians identifying Jesus as both Lord and Messiah (see Acts 2:36). And, it clouds the amazing realization that Jesus had done something totally unanticipated by rising from the dead. We will develop this idea in the resurrection chapter.

As we will soon see, the average Jewish contemporary of Jesus was absolutely convinced he was Messiah. However, that widespread conclusion evaporated rapidly during the trial and crucifixion. Divine? Very few would accept that claim precrucifixion. In fact, the stiff-necked religious leaders crucified Jesus for his "blasphemous" announcement of divinity.

Unlike these contemporaries, we can now benefit from hindsight and see that Jesus presented himself as both Messiah and Lord and backed up that claim through his resurrection. As we develop the theme of Jesus as the divine Messiah, it will become apparent why what we can now see plainly was very hard for Jesus's contemporaries to understand. So as you read on, keep in mind that Jesus was providing evidence that could only be fully understood after that fateful Sunday morning.

Beginning with Moses and the Prophets?

One might think that Jesus would demonstrate his messianic divinity by showing the brutal effects of a crucifixion, but he did not. The Emmaus conversation began with an Old Testament (the only testament of that time) review.

Why would Jesus do that? Stated simply, the Old Testament pays particular attention to a coming Messiah, and the clues given for the identity of this Messiah provide a drawdown argument. In other words, the candidates for Messiah become fewer and fewer as the prophecies progress until, at the end, there is only one credible candidate that can be presented.

What follows is a brief synopsis of a few of the hundreds of Messianic prophecies found in the Old Testament, along with parallel verification in the New Testament. As we said, the argument is a drawdown. That is, each prophecy reduces the candidates for Messiah until only one credible candidate remains.

1. The Messiah would be a man. (We just reduced the sum total of candidates that had lived throughout history by approximately 50 percent.)

   And I will put enmity between you and the woman, and between your offspring and hers; he will crush your head, and you will strike his heel. (Genesis 3:15)
   But when the set time had fully come, God sent his Son, born of a woman, born under the law, to redeem those under the law, that we might receive adoption to sonship. (Galatians 4:4–5)

2. The Messiah would be a Jew from the lineage of Abraham. (Now we have reduced the Messiah to a specific ethnicity and a particular bloodline.)

   Abraham will surely become a great and powerful nation, and all nations on earth will be blessed through him. (Genesis 18:18)

3. And he would be from the lineage of Isaac, which further refines the bloodline.

   Then God said, "Yes, but your wife Sarah will bear you a son, and you will call him Isaac. I will establish my covenant with him as an everlasting covenant for his descendants after him." (Genesis 17:19)

4. And he would also be from the lineage of Jacob, refining the bloodline ever further.

    I see him, but not now; I behold him, but not near. A star will come out of Jacob; a scepter will rise out of Israel. He will crush the foreheads of Moab, the skulls of all the people of Sheth. (Numbers 24:17)

5. And he would be from the tribe of Judah. (The candidates within the Jewish nation's heritage are drawing ever smaller.)

    The sons of Judah: Er, Onan, Shelah, Perez and Zerah (but Er and Onan had died in the land of Canaan). (Genesis 46:12)
    The son of Amminadab, the son of Ram, the son of Hezron, the son of Perez, the son of Judah, the son of Jacob, the son of Isaac, the son of Abraham, the son of Terah, the son of Nahor. (Luke 3:33–34)

6. He would be an heir to the throne of David.

    For to us a child is born, to us a son is given, and the government will be on his shoulders. And he will be called Wonderful Counselor, Mighty God, Everlasting Father, Prince of Peace. Of the greatness of his government and peace there will be no end. He will reign on David's throne and over his kingdom, establishing and upholding it with justice and righteousness from that time on and forever. (Isaiah 9:6–7)
    This is the genealogy of Jesus the Messiah the son of David, the son of Abraham: Abraham was the father of Isaac, Isaac the father of Jacob,

Jacob the father of Judah and his brothers. (Matthew 1:1–2)

7. He would be born in Bethlehem. (Have you ever stopped to consider how few people have been born in Bethlehem? The candidate pool is growing very small.)

But you, Bethlehem Ephrathah, though you are small among the clans of Judah, out of you will come for me one who will be ruler over Israel. (Micah 5:2)
    After Jesus was born in Bethlehem in Judea, during the time of King Herod, Magi from the east came to Jerusalem and asked, "Where is the one who has been born king of the Jews?" (Matthew 2:1–2)

8. He would be born of a virgin. (This claim obviously sounds miraculous, but so does a dead man coming back to life. If the latter is true, there is no reason to doubt the former.)

Therefore, the Lord himself will give you a sign: The virgin will conceive and give birth to a son, and will call him Immanuel. (Isaiah 7:14)
    This is how the birth of Jesus the Messiah came about: His mother Mary was pledged to be married to Joseph, but before they came together, she was found to be pregnant through the Holy Spirit. Because Joseph her husband was faithful to the law, and yet did not want to expose her to public disgrace, he had in mind to divorce her quietly. (Matthew 1:18–19)

9. Infants would be slaughtered. (The Messiah needed to come from a very small town. Additionally, in an act of desperation and in the hope of killing the Messiah before

he could fulfill his destiny, the slaughter of small children took place.)

A voice is heard in Ramah, mourning and great weeping, Rachel weeping for her children and refusing to be comforted, because they are no more. (Jeremiah 31:15)

When Herod realized that he had been out-witted by the Magi, he was furious, and he gave orders to kill all the boys in Bethlehem and its vicinity who were two years old and under, in accordance with the time he had learned from the Magi. Then what was said through the prophet Jeremiah was fulfilled: "A voice is heard in Ramah, weeping and great mourning, Rachel weeping for her children and refusing to be com-forted, because they are no more." (Matthew 2:16–18)

10. The surviving infant would escape to Egypt.

When Israel was a child, I loved him, and out of Egypt I called my son. (Hosea 11:1)

When they had gone, an angel of the Lord appeared to Joseph in a dream. "Get up," he said, "take the child and his mother and escape to Egypt. Stay there until I tell you, for Herod is going to search for the child to kill him." So he got up, took the child and his mother during the night and left for Egypt, where he stayed until the death of Herod. And so was fulfilled what the Lord had said through the prophet: "Out of Egypt I called my son." (Matthew 2:13–14)

11. He would minister in Galilee.

Nevertheless, there will be no more gloom for those who were in distress. In the past he humbled the land of Zebulun and the land of Naphtali, but in the future he will honor Galilee of the nations, by the Way of the Sea, beyond the Jordan—the people walking in darkness have seen a great light; on those living in the land of deep darkness a light has dawned. (Isaiah 9:1–2)

When Jesus heard that John had been put in prison, he withdrew to Galilee. Leaving Nazareth, he went and lived in Capernaum, which was by the lake in the area of Zebulun and Naphtali—to fulfill what was said through the prophet Isaiah: "Land of Zebulun and land of Naphtali, the Way of the Sea, beyond the Jordan, Galilee of the Gentiles—the people living in darkness have seen a great light; on those living in the land of the shadow of death a light has dawned." (Matthew 4:12–16)

12. He would be a prophet like Moses.

The Lord your God will raise up for you a prophet like me from among you, from your fellow Israelites. You must listen to him. For this is what you asked of the Lord your God at Horeb on the day of the assembly when you said, "Let us not hear the voice of the Lord our God nor see this great fire anymore, or we will die." The Lord said to me: "What they say is good. I will raise up for them a prophet like you from among their fellow Israelites, and I will put my words in his mouth. He will tell them everything I command him." (Deuteronomy 18:15–18)

After the people saw the sign Jesus per-
formed, they began to say, "Surely this is the
Prophet who is to come into the world." (John
6:14)

13. He would be a priest like Melchizedek.

The Lord has sworn and will not change his
mind: You are a priest forever, in the order of
Melchizedek. (Psalm 110:4)
    We have this hope as an anchor for the
soul, firm and secure. It enters the inner sanctuary behind the curtain, where our forerunner,
Jesus, has entered on our behalf. He has become
a high priest forever, in the order of Melchizedek.
(Hebrews 6:19–20)

14. He would be rejected by his fellow Jews.

He was despised and rejected by mankind, a
man of suffering, and familiar with pain. Like
one from whom people hide their faces he was
despised, and we held him in low esteem. (Isaiah
53:3)
    He came to that which was his own, but his
own did not receive him. (John 1:11)

15. He would have a manner of triumphal entry.

Rejoice greatly, Daughter Zion! Shout, Daughter
Jerusalem! See, your king comes to you righteous
and victorious, lowly and riding on a donkey, on
a colt, the foal of a donkey. (Zechariah 9:9)
    The next day the great crowd that had come
for the festival heard that Jesus was on his way
to Jerusalem. They took palm branches and went

out to meet him, shouting: Hosanna! Blessed is he who comes in the name of the Lord! Blessed is the king of Israel!" Jesus found a young donkey and sat on it, as it is written: "Do not be afraid, Daughter Zion; see, your king is coming, seated on a donkey's colt." (John 12:12–15)

16. He would be betrayed by a friend.

Even my close friend, someone I trusted, one who shared my bread, has turned against me. (Psalm 41:9)
    Then Judas Iscariot, one of the Twelve, went to the chief priests to betray Jesus to them. They were delighted to hear this and promised to give him money. So he watched for an opportunity to hand him over. (Mark 14:10–11)

17. He would be betrayed for thirty pieces of silver.

I told them, "If you think it best, give me my pay; but if not, keep it." So they paid me thirty pieces of silver. And the Lord said to me, "Throw it to the potter"—the handsome price at which they valued me! So I took the thirty pieces of silver and threw them to the potter at the house of the Lord. (Zechariah 11:12–13)
    Then one of the Twelve—the one called Judas Iscariot—went to the chief priests and asked, "What are you willing to give me if I deliver him over to you?" So they counted out for him thirty pieces of silver. From then on Judas watched for an opportunity to hand him over. (Matthew 26:14–16)

18. His traitor would have the money returned.

I told them, "If you think it best, give me my pay; but if not, keep it." So they paid me thirty pieces of silver. And the Lord said to me, "Throw it to the potter"—the handsome price at which they valued me! So I took the thirty pieces of silver and threw them to the potter at the house of the Lord. (Zechariah 11:12–13)

When Judas, who had betrayed him, saw that Jesus was condemned, he was seized with remorse and returned the thirty pieces of silver to the chief priests and the elders.

"I have sinned," he said, "for I have betrayed innocent blood."

"What is that to us?" they replied. "That's your responsibility."

So Judas threw the money into the temple and left. Then he went away and hanged himself. The chief priests picked up the coins and said, "It is against the law to put this into the treasury, since it is blood money. So they decided to use the money to buy the potter's field as a burial place for foreigners. (Matthew 27:3–7)

19. He would be tortured.

I offered my back to those who beat me, my cheeks to those who pulled out my beard; I did not hide my face from mocking and spitting. (Isaiah 50:6)

They all condemned him as worthy of death. Then some began to spit at him; they blindfolded him, struck him with their fists, and said, "Prophesy!" And the guards took him and beat him. (Mark 14:64–65)

20. He would be hated without cause.

> Those who hate me without reason outnumber the hairs of my head; many are my enemies without cause, those who seek to destroy me. I am forced to restore what I did not steal. (Psalm 69:4)
>
> Whoever hates me hates my Father as well. If I had not done among them the works no one else did, they would not be guilty of sin. As it is, they have seen, and yet they have hated both me and my Father. But this is to fulfill what is written in their Law: "They hated me without reason." (John 15:23–25)

21. He would suffer on our behalf.

> Surely he took up our pain and bore our suffering, yet we considered him punished by God, stricken by him, and afflicted. But he was pierced for our transgressions, he was crushed for our iniquities; the punishment that brought us peace was on him, and by his wounds we are healed. (Isaiah 53:4–5)
>
> When evening came, many who were demon-possessed were brought to him, and he drove out the spirits with a word and healed all the sick. This was to fulfill what was spoken through the prophet Isaiah: "He took up our infirmities and bore our diseases." (Matthew 8:16–17)

22. He would be crucified with sinners.

> Therefore, I will give him a portion among the great, and he will divide the spoils with the strong, because he poured out his life unto death

and was numbered with the transgressors. For he bore the sin of many, and made intercession for the transgressors. (Isaiah 53:12)

Two rebels were crucified with him, one on his right and one on his left. (Matthew 27:38)

23. He would have his hands and feet pierced.

Dogs surround me, a pack of villains encircles me; they pierce my hands and my feet. All my bones are on display; people stare and gloat over me. (Psalm 22:16–17)

Then he said to Thomas, "Put your finger here; see my hands. Reach out your hand and put it into my side. Stop doubting and believe." (John 20:27)

24. He would have his clothes divide at crucifixion by casting lots.

They divide my clothes among them and cast lots for my garment. (Psalm 22:18)

When they had crucified him, they divided up his clothes by casting lots. (Matthew 27:35)

25. He would be mocked with Old Testament words by Old Testament experts.

"He trusts in the Lord," they say, "let the Lord rescue him. Let him deliver him, since he delights in him." (Psalm 22:8)

"He saved others," they said, "but he can't save himself! He's the king of Israel! Let him come down now from the cross, and we will believe in him. He trusts in God. Let God rescue him now if he wants him, for he said, 'I am the Son of God.'" (Matthew 27:42–43)

26. He would resurrect.

> Therefore, my heart is glad and my tongue rejoices; my body also will rest secure, because you will not abandon me to the realm of the dead nor will you let your faithful one see decay. (Psalm 16:9–10)
>
> The angel said to the women, "Do not be afraid, for I know that you are looking for Jesus, who was crucified. He is not here; he has risen, just as he said. Come and see the place where he lay." (Matthew 28:5–6)

Summary of Prophecies

- As we can see, the Messiah must be male.
- Not just any man, but a man of a certain Jewish lineage.
- That lineage must be combined with a certain place of birth (not to mention an unusual parental lineage), and that birth must be accompanied by the slaughter of innocent babies.
- The surviving child's family must flee to Egypt.
- The child, now matured, must be recognized as a prophet greater than Moses, the Patriarch of Israel and the most revered prophet of the Jewish nation.
- The Messiah must be recognized as blameless and, after a short ministry in Galilee, then be scorned by his countrymen.
- He must arrange for a donkey to carry him into Jerusalem, and then persuade the authorities to kill him via the specific manner of crucifixion.
- He also needed criminals to be crucified at his side.

- We should also mention other specifics, such as the request for water that was replaced by gall, the unusual foregoing of breaking the victim's forelegs to hasten death, or the piercing of his side to confirm death.

If This Were a Conspiracy, It Was a Whopper!

All these precise details had to be worked out beforehand if Jesus was an impostor posing as the Messiah. Perhaps most importantly, in order to perpetuate the manufactured lie about his identity, Jesus would have to concoct a plan to have his body removed from the tomb so his followers could later claim they had indeed followed the true Messiah, who was also Lord.

All that would be tough enough, but somehow Jesus must also devise a means to convince multiple audiences, on multiple occasions, they had really seen the resurrected Christ. As we shall soon see, not only would all these things have to be accomplished through conspiracy, but also, the notion of a resurrected Messiah would have been absolutely beyond any belief or expectation of Jesus's contemporaries.

Even the most paranoid conspiracy theorist would have to admit that fabricating these details requires a stretch of credibility. Joseph and Mary would have to be the original conspirators, and they would have to decide to start the process by claiming a virgin birth, then head to Bethlehem for the appropriate place of birth. Somehow Herod would have to be convinced that these two folks were in fact the mother and earthly father of the Messiah, and order children killed in order to eliminate any future threat of a surviving Messiah.

Jesus would then have to buy the whole story that he was the Messiah and agree to remain in the area of Galilee, speaking boldly about the kingdom of God and somehow figuring out a way to change water into wine, heal the sick, raise the dead, and walk on water. Or, at the very least, convince folks he had done all these things and more.

Having played the game to this point, Jesus would then know that he would be proven a fake if he could not demonstrate that he resurrected from the dead, even though we would soon see that there was virtually no understanding of a single man resurrecting, before the end of time, until the resurrection of Christ. In other words, Jesus had to create a PR campaign that would far surpass his death and indeed would remain in place over two thousand years later.

The conspiracy theorist's task is daunting while the rational believer's task is very simple. The profile of the Messiah was made clear via Old Testament prophecies, and they were so specific that any possible candidates would ultimately wither under scrutiny until only one possible Messiah remained standing.

No wonder Jesus began his apologetic for his divinity with Moses and the prophets. He knew the evidence was absolutely over-whelming and, unlike his physical appearances, something that was not contingent upon eye witnesses. Make no mistake, the eyewitness accounts are also crucial to Jesus's claim to divinity, but we believe they are purposefully complementary to the words of the prophets who pointed to the day when God would walk as man on earth.

It is also important to remember how hated by those who were in power Jesus had become. Certainly they thought his death would be the last word on the matter, and one can only imagine their shock and incredulity when his little band of followers began to announce his resurrection.

Rest assured his enemies would have produced whatever proof might have been available to shut this movement down. Yet none was forthcoming, and the skeptic is left to ponder why that is while the believer rests in the knowledge that no proof was forthcoming because none was available.

A few years ago there was a fair amount of hubbub raised by The Jesus Seminar. The group's founder is Dominic Crossan, a New Testament theologian who rejects the literal resurrection of Christ. The Jesus Seminar would display text attributed to Jesus in the Gospels and after some discussion would vote to determine whether the text was accurate. If the Seminar voted the text out, it was considered illegitimate.[2]

Voting on matters such as these strike us as a very poor way of doing academic work. And it exposes biases that will not allow the Bible to be considered as a valid historical document.

There are numerous counters to these biases, and one excellent place to begin would be N. T. Wright's comprehensive work *The Resurrection of the Son of God*.[3] Wright's book is an exhaustive analysis of why we can view the New Testament as a valid historical document, and his arguments are powerful.

That said, we do want to note that it is indeed insufficient to tell a skeptic that "the Bible says it and I believe it." But it is just as wrong for a skeptic à la Crossan to say that Jesus cannot be divine; therefore, he is not divine. Neither position actually examines evidence, so it is evidence that we now return to, beginning with John 8.

Case 1: John 8

We pick up John 8 at the end of the chapter. It is a fascinating discourse, and you should take the time to read the whole exchange that occurred between Jesus and the Jewish crowd. The problem really began when Jesus claimed that he was "the light of the world."

The Pharisees correctly noted that Jewish law required two witnesses to validate a point, and Jesus began to give an explanation of his lineage by noting that he stood with the Father who sent him. At this point in the conversation, things were getting a little prickly as we can see from the following exchange.

Jesus's Claims about Himself

> The Jews answered him, "Aren't we right in saying
> that you are a Samaritan and demon-possessed?"

---

[2]   Pirsen A. Birgsen, "The Gospel According to the Jesus Seminar," October 5, 2016, http://www.veritas-ucsb.org/library/pearson/seminar/js1.html

[3]   Wright, N.T. *The Resurrection of the Son of God*. Minneapolis: Fortress Press, 2003.

"I am not possessed by a demon," said Jesus, "but I honor my Father and you dishonor me. I am not seeking glory for myself; but there is one who seeks it, and he is the judge. Very truly I tell you, whoever obeys my word will never see death."

At this they exclaimed, "Now we know that you are demon-possessed! Abraham died and so did the prophets, yet you say that whoever obeys your word will never taste death. Are you greater than our father Abraham? He died, and so did the prophets. Who do you think you are?"

Jesus replied, "If I glorify myself, my glory means nothing. My Father, whom you claim as your God, is the one who glorifies me. Though you do not know him, I know him. If I said I did not, I would be a liar like you, but I do know him and obey his word. Your father Abraham rejoiced at the thought of seeing my day; he saw it and was glad."

"You are not yet fifty years old," they said to him, "and you have seen Abraham!"

"Very truly I tell you," Jesus answered, "before Abraham was born, I am!" At this, they picked up stones to stone him, but Jesus hid himself, slipping away from the temple grounds. (John 8:48–59)

You get stoned for blasphemy, and the Jews clearly understood Jesus to be equating himself with God, the highest form of blasphemy. We have a clear example of Jesus claiming to be divine here but this is only one example. We now turn to Matthew 9 and pick up the text at verse 4.

Case 2: Matthew 9

> Knowing their thoughts, Jesus said, "Why do you
> entertain evil thoughts in your hearts? Which is
> easier: to say, 'Your sins are forgiven,' or to say,
> 'Get up and walk?' But I want you to know that
> the Son of Man has authority on earth to forgive
> sins." So he said to the paralyzed man, "Get up,
> take your mat and go home." (Matthew 9:4–6)

Something very interesting just occurred. The crowd had
teachers of the Law, better known as scribes, and they studied at the
feet of rabbis as part of their training and repeated the Law until
it was branded in their minds. Indeed, according to Smith's Bible
Dictionary, the "words of the scribes" were sometimes honored above
the Law itself and the scribes were not happy with what happened.
Healing was messianic, and the scribes would be able to recite Isaiah
35:5–6 from memory:

> Then will the eyes of the blind be opened
> and the ears of the deaf unstopped.
> Then will the lame leap like a deer,
> and the mute tongue shout for joy.
> Water will gush forth in the wilderness
> and streams in the desert

Jesus recognized that the scribes were rumbling about what had
just happened. The fact that the crippled man was lowered through a
hole in the roof probably soured their mood, and they were spoiling
for a fight because their thunder had been stolen and any rabbis who
were present were overlooked. Here was a chance to set this fellow
right, or so they thought.

However, Jesus did not duck the scribes' indignant response to
what had happened. Undoubtedly they were prepared to crank out
learned protests to his actions, but they never got the chance. Jesus

seized the moment to declare his divinity by declaring: "Which is easier, to say your sins are forgiven or to say to get up and walk?"

Forgiving sins is an act of God, and the healing of the cripple would be a direct affirmation of Isaiah 35. Jesus pressed on: "To show that I have authority to forgive sin, I command you to get up and go home."

Matthew went on to record that the crowd was filled with awe and praised God for giving such authority to a man. Now that's interesting, isn't it? Jesus had, in the eyes of the scribes, just committed blasphemy, and we know what kind of response blasphemy draws. But it is hard to call it blasphemy when a crippled man heads home after a Jesus encounter.

Case 3: Mark 14

Then, we have this scene: It is the trial of Jesus just prior to his crucifixion. The Jewish leaders were searching for a verdict that would justify death. Jesus gave it to them. Mark 14:55–64 described the events.

> The chief priests and the whole Sanhedrin were looking for evidence against Jesus so that they could put him to death, but they did not find any. Many testified falsely against him, but their statements did not agree. Then some stood up and gave this false testimony against him: "We heard him say, 'I will destroy this temple made with human hands and in three days will build another, not made with hands.'" Yet even then their testimony did not agree.
>
> Then the high priest stood up before them and asked Jesus, "Are you not going to answer? What is this testimony that these men are bringing against you?" But Jesus remained silent and gave no answer. Again the high priest asked him, "Are you the Messiah, the Son of the Blessed One?"

WADE SMITH, PHD AND KEVIN MCKEE, D. MIN.

> "I am," said Jesus. "And you will see the Son of Man sitting at the right hand of the Mighty One and coming on the clouds of heaven."
>
> The high priest tore his clothes. "Why do we need any more witnesses?" he asked. "You have heard the blasphemy. What do you think?"

"What do you think?" That is a good question. What do you think about Jesus's divinity? Did he make compelling claims or should his words be voted out by a seminar? The evidence is powerful but we have more. If someone is still not persuaded that Jesus understood himself to be divine, we have this explanation from N. T. Wright.

Case 4: A Jewish Perspective for the Messiah

N. T. Wright is a prominent British theologian and the former bishop of Dunham. Wright is also a prolific writer and a prodigious scholar. In the appendix of Antony Flew's book *There Is a God*, Wright provides an intriguing way of recognizing Christ's divinity. Wright puts it this way: "My faith in Jesus as the incarnate Son of God does not rest on the verses in the Gospels making this claim. It goes much deeper, in fact way back to the very important question about how first-century Jews understood God and God's action in the world."[4]

At first blush, Wright's statement has some shock value. His faith in Jesus as the incarnate Son of God does not rest on the verses in the Gospels making this claim. How can that be? First of all, Wright is not suggesting that the Gospels are unreliable. What he is saying is that a correct cultural understanding of the times leads to a striking assertion for Christ's divinity that is independent of the Gospel claims regarding Jesus's *possible* divinity.

Wright argues that there are five ways of speaking about God's action in the world, and these actions were all present and active in Jesus. Specifically, they were the following: (1) the Word of God, (2)

---

[4]   Flew, Antony, and Roy Abraham. Varghese. *There Is a God: How the World's Most Notorious Atheist Changed His Mind.* New York: HarperOne, 2008.

the wisdom of God, (3) the glory of God (closely aligned with the temple), (4) the spirit of God, and (5) the law of God.

The Word of God

First-century Jews talked about the Word of God where God speaks and it happens. "Let there be light" from Genesis would be an example of how a contemporary of Jesus would understand God revealing himself through the Word.

Isaiah 55:10–11 provides another example:

> As the rain and the snow
> come down from heaven,
> and do not return to it
> without watering the earth
> and making it bud and flourish,
> so that it yields seed for the sower and
> bread for the eater,
> so is my word that goes out from my
> mouth:
> It will not return to me empty,
> but will accomplish what I desire
> and achieve the purpose for which I sent it.

The Wisdom of God

The Old Testament is replete with scripture that references God's wisdom. Here are a few examples:

- Psalm 111:10—The Lord is the beginning of wisdom.
- Jeremiah 10:12—He founded the world by his wisdom.
- Proverbs obviously spent a great deal of time on wisdom:

> Keep falsehood and lies far from me; give me only poverty nor riches, but only give me my daily bread. Otherwise, I may have too much and disown you and say, "Who is the Lord?" Or

I may become poor and steal and so dishonor the
name of my God. (Proverbs 30:8–9)

God's wisdom was a near universal theme throughout the Old
Testament, and Jesus was quite comfortable in dispensing wisdom.
He talked about the foolish man who built the house on sand and the
wise man who built on a rock. Then, he did something extraordinary
by noting that the wise man was the one who heard these words of
mine and did them. Jesus was not just telling stories; he was declaring
that he is wisdom incarnate.

The Temple of God

The temple was the site that first-century Jews looked to as
the place where God resided. Jesus behaved as if he was the temple.
When Jesus told people their "sins are forgiven," that would have
been a total shock because the temple was where that happened, after
a sacrifice. Jesus declared that you did not have to go to the temple
because essentially the temple had come to them.

We also have the compelling exchange with Jews after Jesus had
cleared the temple in John 2: "What gives you the right to do these
things and what can you do to prove you have the authority?"

Good question, seeing as how Jesus had just wreaked havoc,
but Jesus did not blink at the question. He told them to destroy the
temple, and he would rebuild it in three days. His protagonists did
not understand that he was not referring to a building but rather to
himself. Nevertheless, the challenge was answered in such a way that,
regardless of their understanding of his words, it was clear that Jesus
was acting as God.

The Law of God

The Law had governed Israel's relationship with God since the
days of Moses. It set apart the people of Israel to the God of Israel,
and it was immutable. Yet Jesus had no reservations about not only
interpreting the Law, but also changing it altogether. "You have
heard it said, but I say…" Jesus provided his own unique spin to
centuries-old dictates.

Jesus did something even more remarkable when he gave a new commandment: "Today I give a new commandment, that you love one another as I have loved you." Changing the Law was not a prerogative of man; it was entirely God's purview. Yet Jesus created a commandment, a Law. This language would have shouted to a first-century Jew that Jesus was behaving identically to the way that God acts.

The Spirit of God

The spirit of God is what makes the prophets, prophets. The spirit of God rushed upon Samson in Judges, and the spirit of God was routinely noted as allowing humans to do extraordinary things for God's glory (e.g., Moses). Jesus knew the connection between the spirit of God and the kingdom of God. In fact, he specifically referenced the connection when he said: "If I, by the spirit of God, cast out demons, then the kingdom of God has come upon you."

Jesus Did Not View Himself as Divine?

If Jesus did not view himself as divine, he sure was talking and acting in strange ways. His actions and words shouted to his Jewish contemporaries that Jesus viewed himself as very special. It is indeed interesting that one criticism of Jesus is that he never claimed to be divine. Yet we have seen this is simply not the case. He claimed to be divine, he acted like he was divine, and he spoke in ways that would document he was divine. Jesus was either deluded, or he was divine.

He asked his disciple Peter, "Who do you think I am?" Peter concluded that Jesus was Messiah, and Jesus told him it was because his Father in heaven had helped him reach that decision. The question Jesus asked of Peter is also asked of each of us. Who do you think he is?

Of course, the ultimate claim to divinity rests in the resurrection. The resurrection is the lynchpin for all scripture. Paul understood this when he wrote that we are to be the most pitied if there was no resurrection because our faith would be in vain. So it is to the resurrection that we will shortly turn. However, before we do that, we have one last thought, and this, too, speaks powerfully to Jesus's divinity.

WADE SMITH, PHD AND KEVIN MCKEE, D. MIN.

What Happened?

Have you ever wondered how a crowd could welcome Jesus on his triumphal entry, shout "Hosanna to the highest," and a mere five days later, demand that Barabbas be released because "we have no king but Caesar"?

The response of the Jews to Jesus entering Jerusalem offers a significant clue. They were waving palm branches in remembrance of a great victory by Jews who were opposing Greek influences sometime around the second century BC. The Book of 1 Maccabees chronicled the events of that time, and in chapter 13:51, we find the following:

> And they entered into it the three and twentieth day of the second month, in the year one hundred and seventy-one, with thanksgiving, and branches of palm trees, and harps, and cymbals, and psalteries, and hymns, and canticles, because the great enemy was destroyed out of Israel.

Those welcoming Jesus were also shouting specific verses from Psalm 118. Psalm 118 is a continuous praise of God's love and Israel's dependence upon God. The Psalm also detailed a defender of Israel, one who would cut down her enemies:

> All the nations surrounded me,
> but in the name of the Lord I cut them
>   down.
> They surrounded me on every side,
> but in the name of the Lord I cut them
>   down.
> They swarmed around me like bees,
> but they were consumed as quickly as
>   burning thorns;
> in the name of the Lord I cut them down.
>   (Psalm 118:10–12)

The Psalm also noted a great celebration because of this protector:

> Shouts of joy and victory
> resound in the tents of the righteous:
> "The Lord's right hand has done mighty
>   things!
> The Lord's right hand is lifted high;
> the Lord's right hand has done mighty
>   things!" (Psalm 118:15–16)

Then we see the words that greeted Jesus in verse 26: "Blessed is he who comes in the name of the Lord." Remembrance of a past victory, celebrated with palm shoots and shouts from a psalm of deliverance, leaves no doubt what was happening. In the eyes of the people, *Messiah has come!* And in their view, this meant he was here to deliver them from Roman occupation, provide for God-given justice, and restore the temple to its rightful place as the house of God.

Scripture tells us something markedly different occurred though. Jesus did clear the temple, but he cleared it of his countrymen making money. Roman oppression was certainly not banished in Jesus's last week. In fact, it was on brutal display in Jesus's trial and crucifixion.

How could the Messiah, the anointed one of God, a King who would institute justice on earth, be arrested and subjected to such cruelty? In the eyes of those gathered in Jerusalem for Passover, he could not. Hopes dashed, they turned their wrath on this impostor, demanding a criminal be released instead. After all, Barabbas had at least caused enough problems for the Romans that they had him arrested. Jesus?

"We have no king but Caesar!" cried the mob, in the ultimate insult to the Son of God.

However, their actions are not hard to understand. The disciples themselves did not grasp that Jesus would suffer and die even though he had clearly told them this would happen, so it is easy to see how those on the fringe of Jesus's world would not understand what was happening. As we will see in the resurrection chapter, the idea of a dying Messiah was never considered possible. Yet it quickly became the stated belief of his closest allies.

Summary

Before we travel to those three fateful days, we point out once again that anyone who asks whether Christ knew himself to be divine asks a question that history has irrevocably answered. Christ thought he was divine, Christ acted as if he was divine, and he did things that would have told his contemporaries that he was the promised one. The Jewish religious leaders understood his claim to be divine, and they plotted to kill him as a result. Those present in Jerusalem sincerely believed that Jesus was God's anointed King, so much so that they prepared a Messiah's welcome for his last entry into Jerusalem.

Finally, we have the retrospective of Old Testament messianic prophecy that pointed to Jesus as the anointed one. As we shall soon see, the Messiah did not behave as a Messiah was expected to behave, and he certainly didn't accomplish what was anticipated from him. But, as we shall also soon see, that thinking quickly changed after a rather remarkable weekend of events.

Okay, Jesus thought he was divine, and the people of Israel thought he was Messiah, at least until he was arrested. The only way that Jesus could come to be known as Lord and Messiah would be to demonstrate the ability to conquer death, something that only God himself could do. Jesus in the tomb? We might have a shrine. Empty tomb? We got ourselves a resurrection revolution.

Further Reflection

Central theme: If Jesus Christ is God in the flesh, we should see clear evidence that he and he alone can claim divinity. If we see that, then we have credible reason to understand that the Creator of the universe and God the Father are one and the same.

Reflective Activities

1. Review the Messianic prophecies in the OT provided in your course materials (a very short grouping of many more prophecies). Do the prophecies point to Christ and Christ alone?

2. According to N. T. Wright, a contemporary of Jesus would have understood God to be active in the following ways:
   a) The Word of God
   b) The wisdom of God
   c) The temple of God
   d) The law of God
   e) The spirit of God

3. Why did Jesus's actions incite the Pharisees to plot to crucify him?

4. What was the significance of palm branches and quoting of Psalm 118 in the triumphal entry?

5. What example(s) are in your reading that document that Jesus acted as if he were divine?

6. From the Jewish perspective of Jesus's contemporaries, what was the Messiah's role? Why were the disciples and the community at large unable to grasp the idea that Jesus was both Lord and Messiah?

7. What would be the ultimate declaration of Jesus's divinity?

Chapter 4

Resurrection

> If Jesus rose from the dead, then you have to accept all that he said. If he didn't rise from the dead, then why worry about any of what he said? The issue on which everything hangs is not whether or not you like his teaching, but whether or not he rose from the dead.[1]

The followers of Christ were crushed. Believed to be the Messiah, he had apparently been just another pretender destroyed by the Roman Empire and the religious powers of the day. He was dead, and there was no doubt about it.

His body had been removed from the cross and prepared hurriedly for burial so that no one would be unclean for the Passover. Some of the women who were his disciples came to finish the burial process on Sunday, and the Bible records a rather curious set of events from that point on.

It is absolutely critical to understand the state of mind of those who had believed Christ to be Messiah. From their immediate frame of reference on Friday, this no longer seemed possible. The closest followers of Jesus never understood that the Messiah would suffer

---

[1]   Keller, Timothy. *The Reason for God: Belief in an Age of Skepticism*. New York: Dutton, 2008.

and die. Jesus explained it to them more than once, but they simply could not make the connection.

There are two really good reasons why this is the case: (1) the beliefs of a first-century Jew regarding resurrection and (2) misperceptions about how the Messiah would rule.

The Beliefs of a Second Temple Jew Regarding Resurrection

William Lane Craig in *On Guard: Defending Your Faith with Reason and Precision*[2] and N. T. Wright in *The Resurrection of the Son of God*[3] both make the case that a contemporary of Jesus would have understood resurrection to be something that occurred at the end of time for all mankind. There simply was no expectation of a single resurrection of a single person. Also, and importantly, resurrection was not viewed as "you die and go to heaven." Resurrection meant that there was a life after death. In other words, resurrection required a physical body, and there was an interim time where the spirit was separated from the body.

Wright also noted there was a strong belief that resurrection would be associated with a physical copy of the body, while another school of thought looked at Daniel 12 and concluded that the resurrected body of the righteous would shine like a star. Whatever the thinking of that time, it assuredly did not include the circumstances associated with Jesus's death.

A Second Temple Jew did not believe the Messiah would be required to die. Think about that. The thinking was that the Messiah would remove political oppression, restore the temple to its original specifications (not Herod's redo), and reinstitute temple worship with God literally residing in the temple.

Now imagine yourself as a disciple of Christ and bathed in these traditions. You have been waiting for a Messiah. Indeed Israel had been waiting for a Messiah for thousands of years. You have these preconceptions about who the Messiah will be and

---

[2] Craig, William Lane. *On Guard: Defending Your Faith with Reason and Precision.* Colorado Springs, CO: David C. Cook, 2010.

[3] Wright, N.T. *The Resurrection of the Son of God.* Minneapolis: Fortress Press, 2003.

how he will act. These preconceptions have been fueled by rabbis who diligently searched scripture, trying to understand how the Messiah would behave when he appears. Some of the preconceptions were so strong that some read Isaiah 53 and concluded there must be two Messiahs, one that would conquer and one that would suffer.[4]

Little wonder then that John 12:16 reported that. At first his disciples did not understand all this. Only after Jesus was glorified did they realize that these things had been written about him and that these things had been done to him.

The graphic death of Christ would have served to convince Jesus's followers that all was lost. What no one could possibly understand was that those darkest days were the seeds of a revolution. What they surely did not realize was that the revolution would start so soon and in such a dramatic fashion. It takes a resurrection to create this kind of revolution—nothing smaller will suffice. People who were in absolute despair were transformed virtually overnight into the foot soldiers that became the church.

Jesus himself commissioned the disciples, and he also commanded them (Matthew 28.16–20). Jesus also said he left this world so that greater things would occur (John 14:12–17). Finally, showing the utmost confidence in his followers, he announced that hell itself would not prevail against his movement (Matthew 16:18).

These early followers were radicals, willing to risk beatings and rejoice after they happened (Acts 5), or to suffer cruel deaths by stoning (Acts 7). They believed that Jesus was raised from the dead, and they had good reason to do so.

Building the Case for the Resurrection

Something occurred on that Sunday long ago that changed despair and desperation to bewildered delight. Lots of people have advanced alternative theories as to why that "something" could not be a resurrected Christ. In one sense, it is hard to fault them. The

---

[4] Raphael Patai, *The Messiah Texts* (Avon Books, 1979), vii.

Christian faith holds as its central tenet that Jesus Christ, Holy God and wholly man, was brutally murdered on a cross. His remains were placed in a tomb, and we all know the story about how all heaven broke loose early on that fateful Sunday. Nothing about that story that might seem odd to a skeptic, right?

Is there a rational basis for this core belief of Christianity? Do better explanations exist? Answering these questions goes a long way toward validating or discrediting the Christian faith, and to answer them, we move to the New Testament, the primary source of information related to the resurrection.

The scoffer might immediately jump in and cry foul. How can you use the New Testament as a source of information? How can you know those stories are even true? Since the stories are rooted in history, it is possible to look at known details to see whether what is recorded in the Bible is consistent with what was known of the ancient world. Looking at Acts in particular, we find consistent historical reliability, whether it be in the peculiar titles of local officials or historical details such as the routes of the Alexandrian corn fleet.[5] The details found within Acts are historically accurate, but we should not be surprised since Luke told us in Luke 1 he was writing a carefully reconstructed historical account.

The citation above is just one example of a mountain of defense that can be given to the historical nature of the New Testament. Regarding Jesus himself, it is the very rare historian now who tries to argue against his existence.[6] We do not want to belabor this point too long. If you are predisposed to learning more or concerned about the historical reliability of scripture, there is a bounty of helpful materials available.

[5] Colin J. Hemer, *The Book of Acts in the Setting of Hellenistic History*, ed. Conrad H. Gempf (Tubingen: J. C. B. Mohr, 1989).
[6] William Lane Craig, *On Guard: Defending Your Faith with Reason and Precision* (Colorado Springs: David C. Cook Publishing, 2010)

What We Know

1. There was an empty tomb.

All four Gospels reported an empty tomb. We know that Jesus was buried in a marked tomb. Not just a marked tomb but the marked tomb of a wealthy man. And not just a wealthy man but a member of the Sanhedrin, the small group of men in each city responsible for making sure that Jewish law was followed scrupulously.

It would be hard, as some skeptics claim, to imagine a scenario where the women returning to the tomb on Sunday were confused and went to the wrong tomb. That mistake is too easily rectified, and even if it were not, it leaves the inconvenient truth of a corpse in the correct tomb. The refutation of the empty tomb would be remarkably easy if this were the reason the story originated.

2. There were multiple postresurrection reports of Jesus being alive.

Scripture documents numerous appearances of Christ to varying audiences on different days. A timeline is provided below to illustrate this point. Note that the postresurrection appearances of Jesus ranged appearing before a single person to more than five hundred at another occasion. The multiple appearances in multiple contexts create a high level of credibility for their collective accuracy.

Timeline of the Postresurrection Appearances

Easter
    a) Mary Magdalene—John 20:11–18
    b) The "other Mary," Salome, Joanna, and perhaps one or more other women—Matthew 28:1, Mark 16:1, and Luke 24:10
    c) Simon Peter—Luke 24:34, 1 Corinthians 15:5
    d) Cleopas and friend on Emmaus Road—Luke 24:13–27

THE FOUR PILLARS OF CHRISTIANITY

e)   Disciples (without Thomas)—Luke 24:36–43, John 20:19–23

Week After Easter
   f)   Disciples (with Thomas)—John 20:26–29

Next Month or So
   g)   Seven disciples at Sea of Tiberias—John 21:1–23
   h)   Disciples and large gathering in Galilee—Matthew 28:16–17, 1 Corinthians 15:6
   i)   James, half brother of Jesus—1 Corinthians 15:7

Forty Days After Easter
   j)   Disciples—Luke 24:40–53, Acts 1:1–3

3.   Women were the first witnesses to the resurrection.

All four Gospels document that women were the first to discover the empty tomb. Women were not held in high regard in those days. In fact, a Jewish prayer provided in the Talmud thanks God for not making me a woman, slave, or Gentile. No surprise then that women were not considered credible witnesses in legal matters.

What is surprising is the stubborn fidelity found in the Gospels. Why report a story that is sure to create skepticism? If these were myths, then their creation is certainly unusual. Here is an analogy: Given all we know about the assassination of John F. Kennedy, how much weight would a biography of Lee Harvey Oswald have if it asserted that Oswald was actually in the book depository because he heard there would be an attempt on the president's life, and Oswald was really trying to provide security for the president's motorcade? And, to make matters even more complicated, the biography was written by Oswald's sister?

That analogy is not too far removed from scriptural reality. The Jews of Jesus's time would have been embarrassed to report that they were told these things by women, and the very fact that women were responsible for the first reports would have gotten the resurrection argument off to a very poor start. Still, scripture never flinched, and there has to be a reason why this is the case.

4.   There were other appearances.

As the timeline above indicates, there were multiple eye witnesses to Jesus walking among the people during the forty days post resurrection. Peter, Cleopas and his friend, and the disciples, minus Thomas, all received personal visits on Sunday. In the next few days, the disciples and Thomas had a personal encounter, along with Jesus's brother James. The large crowd of over five hundred men spoken of in 1 Corinthians also saw Jesus during this time. Finally, there was a crowd of disciples, and possibly others, at Jesus's ascension.

5.   The empty tomb and the resurrection are inextricably linked.

The empty tomb by itself is a puzzle, and the resurrection stories by themselves might be dismissed as visions. Collectively though, the empty tomb and the resurrection stories provide powerful evidence that the Bible's descriptions of the first Easter are historically accurate.

The resurrection of Jesus was not something that was anticipated. In fact, it was not even considered possible. As we have noted, contemporaries of Jesus—that is, Second Temple Jews, believed resurrection occurred at the end of the age for all men. There was no consideration given to the idea that a single man would resurrect before the end of the age until Jesus was crucified.

6.   Bewildered disciples transform into emboldened witnesses.

Example 1: Peter

A funny thing happened just a few short days after the resurrection. Men who had no clue that Jesus would suffer and die were now preaching boldly that the scriptures had demanded this outcome. When the Holy Spirit arrived at Pentecost, some were amazed since they were hearing their own language from folks that could not speak it moments before. Others were derisive, claiming that the ones speaking in other languages were actually sloppy drunk. One thing for certain, everyone was paying attention to what was happening. It was at that time that Peter began to speak. We pick up his words in verse 22 of the second chapter of Acts:

> Fellow Israelites, listen to this: Jesus of Nazareth was a man accredited by God to you by miracles, wonders and signs, which God did among you through him, as you yourselves know. This man was handed over to you by God's deliberate plan and foreknowledge; and you, with the help of wicked men, put him to death by nailing him to the cross. But God raised him from the dead, freeing him from the agony of death, because it was impossible for death to keep its hold on him. David said about him:

> I saw the Lord always before me.
> Because he is at my right hand,
> I will not be shaken.
> Therefore my heart is glad and my tongue
>   rejoices;
> my body also will rest in hope,
> because you will not abandon me to the
>   realm of the dead,
> you will not let your holy one see decay.
> You have made known to me the paths
>   of life;
> you will fill me with joy in your presence.

> Fellow Israelites, I can tell you confidently that the patriarch David died and was buried, and his tomb is here to this day. But he was a prophet and knew that God had promised him

on oath that he would place one of his descendants on his throne. Seeing what was to come, he spoke of the resurrection of the Messiah, that he was not abandoned to the realm of the dead, nor did his body see decay. God has raised this Jesus to life, and we are all witnesses of it. Exalted to the right hand of God, he has received from the Father the promised Holy Spirit and has poured out what you now see and hear. For David did not ascend to heaven, and yet he said,

The Lord said to my Lord:
Sit at my right hand
until I make your enemies
a footstool for your feet
Therefore let all Israel be assured of this: God has made this Jesus, whom you crucified, both Lord and Messiah. (Acts 2:22–36)

Remember, this is the same Peter who denied Christ multiple times about fifty days before. His words in Acts hardly sound like someone who claimed he never knew Jesus. Also, what do we make of the crowd? Peter said they were complicit in Jesus's death. Undoubtedly, Peter was addressing some in his audience who had demanded Jesus's death only days before. Now, they listen attentively to an explanation of a risen Christ, and we know from Acts that there was an explosion of believers during this immediate time frame.

Why would these people do such an about-face? Certainly, hearing many languages being spoken and understood had something to do with it, but that was merely the opening act for the true topic of discussion—the resurrection of Jesus. What caused a crowd to carefully consider a claim for a resurrection of a single person that they were complicit in executing? Why were so many willing to believe a claim that, until only a few days before, was completely beyond the imagination of everyone present? Maybe, just maybe, it had something to do with the understanding that the claims for the resurrection of Jesus were not contrived.

Whatever happened, it changed Peter irrevocably. Sometime on resurrection day, Peter had made his way to the empty tomb. He knew there were rumors about Jesus's resurrection, but he was still puzzled. Locked away in a safe room and likely fearing what might happen to them, the disciples all had this little encounter as found in Luke 24:

> While they were still talking about this, Jesus himself stood among them and said to them, "Peace be with you."
>
> They were startled and frightened, thinking they saw a ghost. He said to them, "Why are you troubled, and why do doubts rise in your minds? Look at my hands and my feet. It is I myself! Touch me and see; a ghost does not have flesh and bones, as you see I have."
>
> When he had said this, he showed them his hands and feet. And while they still did not believe it because of joy and amazement, he asked them, "Do you have anything here to eat?" They gave him a piece of broiled fish, and he took it and ate it in their presence.
>
> He said to them, "This is what I told you while I was still with you: Everything must be fulfilled that is written about me in the Law of Moses, the Prophets and the Psalms."
>
> Then he opened their minds so they could understand the Scriptures. He told them, "This is what is written: The Messiah will suffer and rise from the dead on the third day, and repentance for the forgiveness of sins will be preached in his name to all nations, beginning at Jerusalem. You are witnesses of these things. I am going to send you what my Father has promised; but stay in the

city until you have been clothed with power from
on high." (Luke 24:36–49)

So now we know why Peter was so quick to go to scripture that
indicated the Messiah must die. It was because Jesus himself went to
these same scriptures and explained to his closest followers what had
actually happened from Friday to Sunday, from the time of Messiah's
death to the resurrection of Messiah, from the bowels of hell to the
clouds of elation.

Recall, just like their Jewish contemporaries, the disciples also
had no understanding of a unique resurrection by one single person
before the end of time. That idea simply was not considered possible,
which explains why even though Peter had met Jesus on Sunday,
he still could not totally comprehend what was actually happening. After the upper room visit, where the whole story regarding the
Messiah's death and resurrection was made clear, we now find Peter
on Pentecost boldly proclaiming this radical shift in beliefs.

Peter's actions are difficult to explain from a skeptical perspective. Why would he be cowering in a room a few weeks prior, trying
to make sense of Jesus's death, and then confidently assert that the
death of Jesus was a foregone conclusion, foretold by scripture? If
the skeptic argues that Peter was not referencing a literal resurrection, that he somehow had a spiritual "aha," then the skeptic must
also realize that "aha" went against centuries of Jewish teaching. Peter
would have been laughed out of town if he tried to build a case for a
resurrection that really was not a resurrection.

Peter made what he wanted to say quite clear: "God has raised
this Jesus to life, and we are all witnesses of it." Peter knew he could
make this statement because there was the small problem of people
conversing in languages they did not know. Anyone who was present
at Pentecost would have been interested in a reason for what was
happening. Pentecost acted as the launching pad for the Holy Spirit,
but it was also a platform where the case for Jesus's resurrection could
be presented. We know from Acts that the message of resurrection
swept through Jerusalem in short order and, "their numbers increased
greatly."

Example 2: James, the Half Brother of Jesus

We imagine it must have been difficult being the half brother of Jesus, particularly in the years of active ministry that are recorded in the Gospels. We get a glimpse of what it must have been like in Mark 3, where Jesus's kin try to get some folks to persuade him to come out of a house by saying his mother and brothers were looking for him.

"Who are my mother and my brothers?" This answer leads to scripture indicating that James and the family had some concerns about Jesus's mental state (see Mark 3).

Yet somehow, this same James is referred to by Paul as a "pillar of the church" in Galatians. Now why would James steadfastly embrace what he first believed to be nonsense? In fact, embrace it to the point that Josephus reports he was martyred for his faith? If anyone knew Jesus, really knew Jesus, it was his half brother James. When you are willing to die for a cause you earlier discounted, and for a half brother you thought might be mentally unstable, something big has indeed happened.

Example 3: Paul—from Terrorist to Apostle

It strikes us that the church tends to underplay Saul's dedication to hunting Christians. From the perspective of Christians, Saul or Paul was a terrorist, ferreting men and women from their homes simply because they were not practicing the Jewish faith. From Saul's perspective, he was doing what God required; these blasphemers were rendering the true faith impure, and as such, they had to be eradicated.

> Then Saul, still breathing threats and murder against the disciples of the Lord, went to the high priest and asked letters from him to the synagogues of Damascus, so that if he found any who were of the Way, whether men or women, he might bring them bound to Jerusalem. (Acts 9:1–2 NKJV)

Saul was a ringleader in the stoning of Stephen. In fact, Acts 8 tells us he held the garments of those who were martyring Stephen and he looked on with approval. Saul was feared by Christians and with good reason. And then, just like Peter and James, something happened to Saul that changed his life forever, and it occurred on a dusty road on the way to Damascus. Skeptics sometime wonder if a person can be changed immediately upon accepting Christ. Saul is a striking example of that possibility.

Scripture said Saul was struck blind and left to answer a very uncomfortable question. Someone wanted to know why Saul was persecuting him. That question must have really stung Saul, because he was on his way with arrest papers from the high priest so that he could detain any who were following Christ. Saul thought his cause just until he heard a voice from heaven.

"Who are you?" Saul asked.

"I am Jesus, whom you are persecuting" was the reply.

It is one thing to realize your cause is wrong. It is another thing to be devoted to your cause and then discover you have been responsible for opposing what you thought you were defending. Saul thought he was pleasing God by rounding up those who believed in a risen Messiah. He had no idea, until he set out for Damascus, that God and Jesus were identical.

Blinded, Saul continued to Damascus where Ananias had learned in a vision that he would be responsible for restoring Saul's sight. Ananias loved God, but he still couldn't resist pointing out to God that Saul was a murderer. Seems like God already knew that, and he was not dissuaded from his plan to use Saul as a mouthpiece to the Gentiles.

Saul's sight was restored, and immediately, he sets out to the synagogue to prove that Jesus is God. He was so effective, the Jewish leaders put a contract for his life on him. Saul's friends learned what was going on and got Saul out of Damascus. Saul returned to Jerusalem where Barnabas acted as his defender to an understandably leery group of apostles. Saul eventually won the trust of the apostles and argued so convincingly for Christ that the Jewish leaders plotted to kill him in Jerusalem as well. Saul, on fire for Christ, escaped

Jerusalem and headed for Tarsus and the beginning of his ministry to the Gentiles.

Saul or Paul?

Acts 13:9 is the first time we learn that Saul has an alias. Saul was also known as Paul. Why did he adopt Paul as his name? Because Paul is the gentile variation of Saul, and Paul knew the Gentiles would be more likely to listen to someone who was one of them. Paul was indeed willing to be all things to all men so that some may come to know that God the Father did in fact send Jesus as God incarnate to save the world from sin (1 Corinthians 9:19–23).

Paul is another inconvenient truth to the skeptic. He was educated, and he was absolutely dedicated to the mission of eradicating the new movement known as the Way. He was a shining example of what a Jew should be—circumcised on the eighth day, of the people of Israel, of the tribe of Benjamin, and a Hebrew of Hebrews. In regard to the law, he was a Pharisee; as for zeal, persecuting the church; as for righteousness based on the law, faultless (Philippians 3:5–6).

All that might have been true, but it was no longer meaningful to Paul. In the very next verse of Philippians, Paul told us that whatever were gained, he now considered them a loss for the sake of Christ. How to account for a man going from murderer to martyr? Paul said he was forever changed in an instant on the road to Damascus. Who would know better? Paul became the most prolific writer in the New Testament, and ultimately, he was beheaded because, as a Roman, he could not be crucified. Paul, writing some of his last words, said this in 2 Timothy 4:

> For I am already being poured out as a drink offering, and the time of my departure has come. I have fought the good fight, I have finished the course, I have kept the faith; in the future there is laid up for me the crown of righteousness, which the Lord, the righteous Judge, will award to me on that day; and not only to me, but also to all

who have loved His appearing. (2 Timothy 4:6–8 NKJV)

Dismissing Paul's testimony to the risen Messiah is difficult to do. Obviously, he was willing to die for his convictions. Just as obvious, his focus changed instantly from persecuting Christians to spreading the gospel. When you add Paul to the mix of evidence that already exists, the conclusion becomes all the more apparent that the Bible is scrupulously recording the most important time in the history of the world.

Maybe All These Stories Are Concoctions Written Well after the Fact

A last recourse left to a skeptic would be to argue that Acts (and therefore the Gospels) were written well after the events described, allowing crazy stories and mythologies to be developed and passed on as true. Men speaking in other languages? Cannot happen, says the skeptic, and therefore a very late date for Acts would mean that these stories have been concocted rather than accurately recorded.

It is important for a follower of Christ to know that the Bible they hold in their hands today did not come from original manuscripts. Nor did it come from copies of original manuscripts, and most likely, it did not come from copies of copies of manuscripts. The earliest agreed upon fragments of scripture came from manuscripts that dated to AD 100–200, although an intriguing find of a papyrus text in a mummy's mask appeared to be a fragment of Mark from the first century, perhaps AD 80. If true, this is a remarkable discovery of a Biblical text likely written by those with firsthand knowledge of the resurrection.[7]

Why would anyone conclude the New Testament is trustworthy if the manuscripts used in its creation are dated well after the actual time of Christ? This is a good question, and it would be

---

[7] Jarus, Owen. "Mummy Mask May Reveal Oldest Known Gospel." *Live Science.* January 18, 2015. https://www.livescience.com/49489-oldest-known-gospel-mummy-mask.html

exceedingly difficult to answer if it were not for the fact that we have so many manuscripts in place. Each time an earlier manuscript has been found, it has been used to fact check the manuscripts that were produced later. Biblical scholar Daniel B. Wallace provides an explanation:

> As with all the previously published New Testament papyri (127 of them, published in the last 116 years), not a single new reading has commended itself as authentic. Instead, the papyri function to confirm what New Testament scholars have already thought was the original wording or, in some cases, to confirm an alternate reading—but one that is already found in the manuscripts. As an illustration: Suppose a papyrus had the word "the Lord" in one verse while all other manuscripts had the word "Jesus." New Testament scholars would not adopt, and have not adopted, such a reading as authentic, precisely because we have such abundant evidence for the original wording in other manuscripts. But if an early papyrus had in another place "Simon" instead of "Peter," and "Simon" was also found in other early and reliable manuscripts, it might persuade scholars that "Simon" is the authentic reading. In other words, the papyri have confirmed various readings as authentic in the past 116 years, but have not introduced new authentic readings. The original New Testament text is found somewhere in the manuscripts that have been known for quite some time.[8]

---

[8] Daniel B. Wallace, https://voice.dts.edu/article/wallace-new-testament-manscript-first-century/

Wallace correctly pointed out that each time we find earlier manuscripts, they endorsed what was written in later manuscripts. This confirms that the copyists paid scrupulous attention to copying the original transcripts as they were originally written. For example, there are over 5,600 Greek manuscripts of the New Testament, with the earliest copies dating to approximately AD 130. When these manuscripts were subjected to the type of analysis just described by Wallace, they exhibited 99.5 percent accuracy. And the minor differences have no consequence on the intent or meaning of the scripture itself. Stated plainly, the manuscripts are incredibly accurate, and our New Testament is indeed reliable.[9]

Dating Acts (and the Gospels and Consequently the New Testament)

Having said all that, what might be reasonable estimates for the original manuscripts for the New Testament? Norman Geisler, arguing for an early dating of Acts in *Baker Encyclopedia of Christian Apologetics*,[10] listed forty-three pieces of evidence that validate that Acts was most likely authored around AD 60–62. Listed below are six of the most important observations from Dr. Geisler.

Reason 1: Details that would not be expected if Acts were written well after the events occurred.

1. The proper river port, Perga, for a ship crossing from Cyprus (13:13)
2. The proper port, Attalia, for returning travelers (14:25)
3. The correct route from the Cilician Gates (16:1)
4. The proper locations where travelers would spend successive nights on this journey (17:1)

---

[9] Slick, Matt. "Manuscript Evidence for Superior New Testament Reliability." *Christian Apologetics & Research Ministry*. December 10, 2008. https://carm.org/manuscript-evidence

[10] Geisler, Norman L. *Baker Encyclopedia of Christian Apologetics*. Grand Rapids, MI: Baker Books, 2006.

5. The correct explanation that sea travel with favoring east winds was the most convenient way to reach Athens in the summer (17:14)
6. The permanent stationing of a Roman cohort in the Fortress Antonia to suppress disturbances at festival times (21:31), the flight of steps used by guards (21:31, 35)

Reason 2: Paul and Peter were still alive in Acts.

Nero began a staggering and systematic elimination of Christians sometime around AD 65. The carnage continued for five years or so until Nero committed suicide in AD 70. Scholars agree that Paul and Peter both were victims of Nero's persecution of Christians. If this were the case, both would have died sometime prior to AD 70. Using that date as the most conservative, that means Acts would have been completed in the early to late sixties, and that agrees with Geisler's conclusions. We can be confident then that the book of Acts dates to sometime prior to AD 70.

Reason 3: Luke was written before Acts.

If Acts dates to the sixties, then Luke must precede Acts since the two were written consecutively. We are now backing up even further toward the crucifixion and resurrection of Christ.

Reason 4: Luke appears to have used Mark as a source.

Most scholars agree that this is the case. If so, it means we are even closer to the resurrection.

Reason 5: You cannot make up stories of this magnitude this close to the actual event.

Myths take time, particularly myths that undo centuries of deeply ingrained beliefs. The only way the stories could be mythologized would be if they were written well after the fact, with considerable license taken in the effort. As we have seen, the attention to scrupulous reproduction of the earliest works has never wavered. There is no evidence of hyperbolic inflation of the claims of the New Testament.

Reason 6: The Gospels operate as independent sources.

Much has been made in modern criticism about what Gospel borrowed from what Gospel and when all these books were actually written. We do not wish to delve too far into this topic, but it is important to point out that, as noted above, Mark is generally accepted as the earliest Gospel written, with Luke using Mark as a source.[11] It is also probable that Matthew used Mark and there is an outside chance that Mark used Matthew.[12]

We think these modern criticisms are interesting but also wildly speculative. Consider how Wright made the case in *The Resurrection of the Son of God.*

> (Speaking of the Gospels and their interdependence)… There is remarkably little verbal overlap. Instead, we find in each of the stories not so much a sign of steady development from a primitive tradition to a form in which the evangelist simply wrote down what the tradition at that point had grown into, but rather a retelling of primitive stories by the evangelist himself in such a way as to form a fitting climax to his particular book. You could not take Luke's ending and substitute it for John's, or John's for Matthew's, without creating an absurdity… The evangelists have exercised considerable freedom in retelling and reshaping the narratives so as to bring out themes and emphases that were important to them throughout their work.

---

[11] Christianity Today reports the oldest known manuscript of Mark has recently been dated between A.D. 150-250 by the Egypt Exploration Society. Details can be found at: https:www.christianitytoday.com/ct/2018/may-web-only/mark-manuscript-earliest-not-first-century-fcm.html

[12] Wright, N.T. *The Resurrection of the Son of God.* Minneapolis: Fortress Press, 2003.

Wright is correct that any effort to explain away the Gospels as similar regurgitated efforts is fraught with issues. The Gospels do not read that way at all. They are unique narratives that tell the same story from differing perspectives. Just as multiple witnesses to a crime might all emphasize certain happenings based upon their perspective, so too the Gospel writers.

The fact that the accounts of Peter's denial differ as to how many times, and when the cock crowed, is not evidence of manufactured stories. Indeed, quite the opposite. If the stories such as Peter's denial and the number of women were manufactured years after the fact, we would expect all the wrinkles to be ironed smooth. There would be no difference in perspectives because all the perspectives would have emanated from one source. But we do not have that with the Gospels. They told their stories from their own perspectives, yet each made the case clear. Jesus rose physically and bodily from a rich man's tomb on the third day.

If the skeptic argues Acts, the Gospels, and indeed the New Testament are late inventions, he must deal with the evidence noted above. He should also remember that it is not possible to concoct myths of this magnitude in such a short time. Especially myths that would completely contradict millennia of Jewish teaching related to resurrection in general and the expected actions of their Messiah in particular.

So now we know that the story of men speaking strange languages was not invented as a myth long after the fact, thereby allowing Jesus's later followers a platform to tell a tale that bore little resemblance to the actual events. No. The story of men speaking strange languages was dutifully recorded by Luke, and it was done in a time frame that placed Acts very close to the actual day Christ left the tomb. The miracle of Pentecost was linked to the miracle of Christ's resurrection in such a way that a Jew of that time would have been able to quickly grasp that the Messiah they had hoped for had indeed arrived.

Reason 7: Resurrection becomes the point of Christianity

Just like today, the early church argued about a lot of stuff—circumcision, Jewish ritual, appropriate behaviors, you name it. There were so many things that were being argued about that a council was set up in Jerusalem to settle matters of doctrine (Acts 15). There was one thing though that the early church never argued about. The resurrection of Christ was a settled matter from the beginning of the Christian movement.

Also, the resurrection of Christ was the absolute centerpiece of the movement. As we detailed earlier, James, Peter, and Paul exhibited remarkable changes in beliefs and behaviors after the crucifixion, and this was undoubtedly based on their unwavering conclusions that Jesus had physically resurrected. The family skeptic, the Messiah's denier, and Jesus's persecutor were all transformed. This is what happens when truth sets in, and the conclusion that Jesus rose from the dead was obviously not limited to these three men. Thousands in Jerusalem began to understand within fifty odd days after Easter that Jesus had to die as the Messiah, and they, too, were transformed. Pentecost flipped the switch on the exponential growth of the church. None of this could have occurred without the resurrection of Christ because the bodily resurrection of Christ was what was preached at Pentecost.

Pentecost is the first time we see meek followers of Christ, lost in doubt and fear on Good Friday, transformed into lions of the faith, boldly proclaiming the truth of Jesus's resurrection. Acts provides multiple examples of this occurring, and every author in the New Testament developed their writings and teachings based on the resurrection of Christ.

Paul minced no words in 1 Corinthians 15:17: "If Christ has not been raised, your faith is futile." The resurrection of Christ was the driving force that fueled the early church, and the resurrection of Christ was the basis for its inception. Unlike Judaism, where resurrection was important but not central, resurrection in the Christian faith became the foundation from which all other facets of the faith developed.

There is no rational explanation for such a marked and immediate shift in the thinking of both the disciples and the people of Jerusalem, except for a steadfast conviction that the resurrection of Jesus had indeed occurred. Christianity was not an evolution of previous beliefs; it was an explosion of a new argument concerning how God would intervene in the affairs of man.

In 1 Corinthians 15:3–4, Paul drew a succinct summary of this radical new movement:

> For what I received I passed on to you as of first importance: that Christ died for our sins according to the Scriptures, that he was buried, that he was raised on the third day according to the Scriptures.

Christ died, he was buried, and he was raised on the third day. All this according to scripture. That is the summation of our faith, and we should appreciate how strong the evidence is supporting these claims.

How Else to Explain All This?

Competing theories attempting to explain the resurrection are bogged down by innumerable difficulties. Suggesting the tomb was not really empty is easily dismissed because of how easy it would be to relocate the actual burial spot. We think it more than likely that the powers of that time would have paraded the body through the streets of Jerusalem to quell the foolishness of a resurrected corpse. But they did not do that, did they?

To argue that the disciples stole the body is to ignore all their words that indicate their absolute insistence that Jesus had physically risen from the dead. This theory requires a collective band of lunatics to replace the otherwise normal disciples that scripture describes.

Suggesting the disciples collectively suffered from posttraumatic stress and that they all saw ethereal visions they interpreted as an actual risen savior is problematic as well. There is no documented case of deluded masses experiencing identical visions, and we cannot think of any way this could ever happen. And once again, if these visions were delusions, it would be really simple to parade the body around town and take care of that problem.

Then we have the women, embarrassments to the story due to their inability to serve as credible witnesses. A myth would not be expected to begin with sources that are so easily discredited. That said, all four Gospels report women as the first to find the empty tomb.

Explaining Saul to Paul is also a difficult task for the skeptic. What possesses a person to claim that they have had a personal visitation from Jesus, especially when this Jesus was precisely the enemy you had been railing against? Saul the murderer to Paul the apostle. The very traits that made Paul so zealous for his religion would later serve him well as he became even more zealous for his savior. Paul's life and death are powerful testaments to his unshakable belief that Jesus was the risen Messiah.

We also have the transformed lives of Peter and James. Both were martyred for their faith, and both provided amazing testimonies that point conclusively to the fact that they were irrevocably convinced that Jesus is Messiah and that he had resurrected bodily from the dead, all according to God's plan.

Then, there was a remarkable exchange in Acts 2. Peter spoke to a large crowd that included actual participants in the courtyard exchange with Pilate that ultimately led to Jesus's crucifixion. These were the same people who thought Jesus was a fake. Their understanding of a Messiah was one who would reestablish proper temple worship while expelling the Roman oppressors. Surely, the man called Jesus did none of these things, and the response of the Jews of that time was swift. But somehow, these same people were now willing to abandon the beliefs held for centuries by their forefathers. Something happened after the crucifixion that caused them to reconsider the very circumstances they believed deserved death just a few days before. What changed their minds?

Finally, we have documented appearances of Jesus coming from multiple sources over multiple days. In some cases, there were very few people present; in others, there were several hundred. In every case, the reports of the postresurrection appearances were never discredited.

Whatever the objection is to the historical reality of the crucifixion and resurrection of Jesus, it is difficult to see how any objection provides greater explanatory power than that proposed by scripture. If one presumes there is no God, then one is obliged to figure out a way to demonstrate that there is also no Son of God. But as we have seen, the evidence for God is compelling and the evidence for the resurrection is equally powerful.

There is still one powerful objection to Christianity and it comes from morality. How can an all-powerful, all-loving God allow evil?

Further Reflection

Central theme: A Second Temple Jew did not believe the Messiah would die. The thinking was that the Messiah would remove political oppression, restore the temple to its original specifications (not Herod's redo), and reinstitute temple worship with God literally residing in the temple.

Reflective Activities

1. How does the skepticism of Second Temple Jews about Jesus's resurrection compare to modern skepticism about the resurrection?
2. How will you respond to a skeptic who says the New Testament is not a historical document?
3. What symbolism is present in the actions of those welcoming Jesus into Jerusalem upon his triumphal entrance?
4. How do the empty tomb and the physical appearances of Jesus combine to create a powerful argument for his physical resurrection?
5. Is there an alternative explanation that better explains the immediate shift in thinking of James, Peter, and Paul regarding Jesus's bodily resurrection?

Chapter 5

What about Suffering?
How Can Evil Exist if God Is
All-Good and All-Powerful?

If God does not exist, then everything is permitted.[1]

A powerful argument against God is the existence of evil. We do not know anyone who would argue that evil is not a problem on this planet. Pick up the paper any day of the week and you will be bombarded by man's inhumanity to man. History reminds us that Hitler was responsible for viciously slaughtering six to seven million victims in the Holocaust. Yet as horrific that number is, it pales in comparison to the twenty million people eradicated by Joseph Stalin's regime.

---

[1] Fyodor Dostoyevsky, *The Brothers Karamazov*. Some ado has been made by skeptics as to whether Dostoyevsky actually wrote the quote so commonly attributed to him. His novel has been translated into many languages from its original Russian, English included. A thorough analysis of the text and its accuracy can be found at http://infidels.org/library/modern/andrei_volkov/ dostoevsky.html. Ironically, the discussion provides a thorough defense for the accuracy of the quote only to later suggest Dostoyevsky did not intend the statement to be interpreted as is common custom. With apologies to Shakespeare: Alas, poor Yorick, we disagree!

Today, we are faced with Al-Qaeda and ISIS, entities that hardly anyone knew about in the western world until 9/11 and subsequent unrest in the Middle East. It seems like the more we progress, the more we are reminded that evil continually lurks and all too often interjects into the affairs of man. Evil has been with us as long as there has been an us.

This reality has led skeptics to posit that evil is evidence that there is no God. Essentially, the argument looks like this:

1. God is all good.
2. God is all loving.
3. An all-loving, all-good God will not allow evil.
4. Evil exists.
5. Therefore, God does not exist.

This attack on God, in our opinion, is one of the most dangerous. It must be answered, and answered well, if the skeptic's understandable concerns will be addressed. Maybe even more important, it must be answered well if we as Christians are not to be doomed to live in constant doubt about whether God is really there and whether he really cares.

Notice the skeptic is basing the whole argument on the existence of evil. Well, what is sauce for the goose is also sauce for the gander. Consider the following counterargument:

1. God is all good.
2. God is all loving.
3. Without God, objective moral values do not exist.
4. Evil exists as an objective moral value.
5. Therefore God exists.

Note the similarity between the two arguments. The big distinction is the way evil is dealt with. The skeptic says that evil cannot exist if God exists. We counter that by noting that evil does exist but cannot do so unless there is a basis for objective moral values.

Without objective moral values, everyone is free to decide for themselves what is and is not evil.[2]

In essence, everyone is free to act as their own god, and if that is the case, then Hitler and Stalin are both free to make their own rules regarding what is and is not evil. Without objective moral values, how will we even know what evil is?

This is not to say that an atheist cannot act in a moral fashion. That line of reasoning is obviously fallacious, and there are innumerable examples that disprove that argument. Atheists can and do behave morally.

However, having said that, it is important to separate a moral behavior from an objective moral reality. Man may interpret what is moral, but man cannot create objective moral values. For every person who says that taking an innocent life is evil, there is an example of a Hitler or Stalin who would argue that the deaths they sanctioned brought about a greater good. From their perspective, those who were killed were inferior or drains upon society.

Who's to say who is right? Suppose Germany had won World War II? Would we hold the same view of evil that we do today? The answer is yes, but only if we hold to an objective moral reality that defines evil independent of the current views of society.

What Is the Source of Evil?

In the skeptical argument against God, evil is viewed as God's responsibility. Either he created evil, or he is impotent to stop its progress. If he created evil, then God is not all-good. If he cannot stop evil, then he is not all-powerful.

But, what if God is not responsible for evil? What if evil derives from another source?

We deny that evil is God's responsibility. God did not create evil because evil is not created. It is a consequence of choice. God will stop evil, but that time is not here yet. There will come a time when

---

[2]   The philosophical argument that objective moral reality is dependent upon a transcendent God can be found in a number of writings. A concise presentation may be found in *On Guard* by William Lane Craig.

there is a new heaven and a new earth, where there is no sorrow or suffering, but that is certainly not the present situation.

Jesus was quite aware of the presence of evil in this world. In John 16:33, Jesus said this: "In this world, you will have troubles. But take heart, I have overcome the world."

What then is the source of these troubles? Many books have been written about the source of evil and how its existence can be reconciled with God. One of the best and most succinct explanations we have seen comes from a book coauthored by Peter Kreeft and Ronald K. Tacelli entitled *Handbook of Christian Apologetics*.[3] We highly recommend the book as a tremendous source for common-sense answers to many difficult questions.

This is how Kreeft and Tacelli make the case:[4]

> To help understand Creation and the Fall, the image of three iron rings suspended from a magnet is helpful. The magnet symbolizes God; the first ring, the soul; the middle ring, the body; and the bottom ring, nature. As long as the soul stays in touch with God, the magnetic life keeps flowing through the whole chain, from divine life to soul life, body life and nature life. The three rings stay harmonized, united, magnetized. But when the soul freely declares its independence from God, when the first iron ring separates from the magnet, the inevitable consequence is that the whole chain of rings is demagnetized and falls apart. When the soul is separated from God, the body is separated from the soul—that is, it dies—and also from nature—that is, it suffers. For the soul's authority over the body is a delegated authority, as is humanity's authority over

---

[3] Kreeft, Peter, and Ronald Tacelli. *Handbook of Christian Apologetics*. Downer's Grove, Illinois: Intervarsity Press, 1994.

[4] Kreeft and Tacelli's book is a very useful tool, covering a wide range of apologetic topics in an easy-to-follow format.

nature. When God the delegator is rejected, so
is the authority he delegated. If you rebel against
the king, his ministers will no longer serve you.
Thus both suffering and sin are traced to man,
not God.[5]

We suggest that you read the above slowly. It is the most succinct and easy to understand explanation for the presence of evil that
we have come upon. The conclusion it draws—namely, that man
is responsible for both sin and suffering—is the biblical worldview.
Man was told that all the perks of Eden were free and readily available. Everything man could want was there, and there was only one
thing man was not supposed to do.

We know the story, but it is important to note something about
human nature at this point. We are inevitably drawn to that which
we are not supposed to be drawn to.

Theologically, this is known as a sin nature. Paul railed against
his own nature in Romans 7, and then reminds himself and all of us
that there is no condemnation for those who are in Christ. None of
us are immune to this disease, and here's a simple proof that we are
all burdened with it: *don't think of the Mona Lisa.*

What, pray tell, was the first thing that came to your mind? It is
impossible not to think of da Vinci's famous painting. So, too, with
sin. When we are told not to do something, our natures immediately
turn to the very thing we are not supposed to do.

Paul spoke clearly of our old sin nature, and how it no longer
holds us in bondage. But as we said, Paul had to remind himself of
that reality, and it is a good thing for us to do so as well. Because
of our sin nature, we now have a world where suffering and sin are
indeed all too real.

---

[5]   Ibid., 135.

James, Paul, Job, and Jesus: Examples of How to Deal with Evil and Suffering

James

The book of James provides this little gem of advice:

> Consider it pure joy, my brothers and sisters, whenever you face trials of many kinds, because you know that the testing of your faith produces perseverance. Let perseverance finish its work so that you may be mature and complete, not lacking anything. (James 1:2–4)

Note that James did not dwell on the nature of the trial itself, but instead was totally focused on the response to it. From James's perspective, the trial was a circumstance that created an opportunity to depend upon the source of faith. James's scripture is totally congruent with Jesus's admonition that we will have troubles in this world, but we should not despair because he has overcome the world.

Paul

In 1 Thessalonians 5, Paul wrote these words:

> Rejoice always, pray continually, give thanks in all circumstances; for this is God's will for you in Christ Jesus. (1 Thessalonians 5:16–18)

Paul, like James and Jesus placed his emphasis on the response to the circumstance not the circumstance itself. Paul was certainly no stranger to circumstances. Note what he wrote to the Philippians:

> I rejoiced greatly in the Lord that at last you renewed your concern for me. Indeed, you were concerned, but you had no opportunity to show it. I am not saying this because I am in need, for I have learned to be content whatever the cir-

cumstances. I know what it is to be in need, and
I know what it is to have plenty. I have learned
the secret of being content in any and every situation, whether well fed or hungry, whether living
in plenty or in want. I can do all this through him
who gives me strength. (Philippians 4:10–13)

Lots of people recite the last words of this passage without giving due thought to the context. Paul was reminding his audience that
the response to the circumstances was far more important than the
actual circumstance. Sound familiar?

And then we have the example from Job:

Job

Job is likely the first recorded psychological field trial to document the source of man's behaviors. Satan posited that Job's dependence upon God could be shattered by manipulating the environment. God allowed the trial to proceed with the condition that Job
could not be killed.

And so, the experiment into man's true nature began. Satan was
certain that Job would curse God if enough bad things happened to
him. It is important to notice in the book of Job that God was, for
the most part, passive. Job constantly reminded himself that God is
worthy of worship after the various calamities struck him, but God
remained quiet. Job's friends opined about all the bad things Job had
done and suggested that he should just curse God, die, and get it over
with. Job 7:20 provided one gut-wrenching example of Job's anguish:

If I have sinned, what have I done to you, O
watcher of men? Why have you made me your
target?

The middle chapters of Job were an ongoing conversation
between Job and his circle of friends. They kept pointing out truths
that Job was well aware of, and then they concluded that Job's situation was a result of something Job did wrong. In chapter 12, it

became clear that Job has had enough of the pandering advice he was getting, and he basically went all in and remarked:

> Men at ease have contempt for misfortune. (Job 12:5)

Job then made some very important observations that flew directly in the face of what his friends were asserting. They kept claiming that something Job did provoked God to create his misery, but Job knew that the truth was far deeper:

> The tents of marauders are undisturbed, and those who provoke God are secure—those who carry their god in their hands. (Job 12:6)

Job then went through a series of scenarios in which he emphasized that God is sovereign and notes that both the deceived and the deceiver are his. Job was building up to a melting point with his friends and their condescending advice.

> What you know I also know; I am not inferior to you. But I desire to speak to the Almighty and to argue my case with God. You however, smear me with lies; you are worthless physicians, all of you! If only you would be altogether silent! For you, that would be wisdom. (Job 13:2–5)

Even in the face of Job's withering rebuke, his friends could not resist further ruminations. Consider Eliphas's reply in chapter 15:

> But you even undermine piety and hinder devotion to God. Your sin prompts your mouth; you adopt the tongue of the crafty. Your own mouth condemns you, not mine; your own lips testify against you. (Job 15:4–6)

Job finally answered all this "advice" with a reply we should all give careful thought to:

> I could also speak like you, if you were in my place; I could make fine speeches against you and shake my head at you. But my mouth would encourage you; comfort from my lips would bring what you need. (Job 16:4–5)

On it went, with the book of Job pointing out that the "friends" were doing nothing more than providing pious patronage of Job the man. They continued to belittle him even after Job called them out for doing so. Back and forth, the argument went until chapter 38, where God showed up.

The Test No One Can Answer

In chapter 38, we heard from God and the questions were direct. "Where were you when I laid the earth's foundations?" was the first question posed to Job, and the ones that followed were not any easier. "Have you ever given orders to the morning or shown the dawn its place?"

These questions were the start of the hardest exam that had ever been given on earth. Chapters 38 and 39 documented fifty odd questions that God asked Job, which could only be answered by God. It does not take a genius to figure out that God was not asking Job questions and expecting answers. God was making a point, and he was doing it in such a way that there would be no doubt as to who was the Creator was and who was the created. The quiz concludes with this command: "Will the one who contends with the Almighty correct him? Let him who accuses God answer him!"

Job's answer to all the questions? "I am unworthy—how can I reply to you? I put my hand over my mouth" (Job 40:3).

What can we learn from Job?

- In the midst of Satan's antics, God remained silent.

- Think about that one for a moment. In all the arguments between Job and his friends, about why all this stuff was happening, God remained silent.
- Just because God was silent does not mean God was indifferent.
- Job refused to let what was happening around him influence what he knew in his heart to be true.
- Job demonstrated definitively that our beliefs about God should not be based upon our circumstances in life.
- Job also clearly noted that many times good things happened to bad people (e.g., Job 12:6).
- Job established clearly that God was more interested in Job's response to the trial than the details of the actual trial itself. Sound familiar?

Many people turn to the end of Job and conclude that the moral of the book is that Job persevered, so he was blessed. That, in our view, is an incorrect reading of the book. Job had no idea that he would ever be restored, so there was no expectation or "name it and claim it" on his part. Job only knew that God was not to be cursed and that the very nature of God was not to be questioned. Job placed his fate in God's hand, not without considerable consternation, but because he knew there was no better option.

There was another event recorded in scripture in which someone placed their life in God's hand, and it was also done with considerable consternation. Once again, the person knew there was no better place to be than with God, regardless of the circumstances. He is Jesus Christ, God in human flesh.

The Gethsemane Prayer

We all know the scene. Hours before his capture and eventual crucifixion, Jesus is alone in the Garden of Gethsemane. He is anguished to the point of torment and torture. Here, we had God talking to God. Jesus spoke his heart. "Abba, everything is possible for you. Take this cup from me" (Mark 14:36).

What a prayer. It was accompanied by such stress that capillaries were rupturing at the skin's surface, flooding layers of skin, and eventually oozing out through pores. Jesus was literally sweating blood. Then, Jesus made a remarkable statement. "Yet not what I will, but what you will."

The most powerful prayer ever uttered in the history of the world was met with "no." Chew on that for a second. God the Father and God the Son spoke in the most poignant conversation ever recorded.

It is crucial to note that the conversation did not end with God's reply. If we leave it there, it sounds like we should be prepared to accept that God will not always do what we want and that is not the point at all, although it is certainly true.

Jesus's answer to God's will is our example to follow. Recognizing the path he would take, Jesus turned to what he knew must be done if man were to ever be able to stand in God's presence. The trial in this case, even a trial as heinous as a crucifixion of the Messiah, is not the main point of the Gethsemane prayer. The main point is that Jesus's response was not to focus on the trial but rather how he should respond to it.

Job also understood that how we respond to the trial is more important than the trial itself. He suffered unspeakable loss, but it is not hard to read Job and conclude that a summation of the book of Job is this—not my will but yours.

Paul was a warrior for Christ, enduring many hardships. He was beat several times, faced hunger, and was imprisoned for his faith. He was ultimately beheaded. It would not be incorrect to read all Paul's writings on trials and sufferings and also note that they can be summarized with the same conclusion—not my will but yours. So, too, for James.

The implications should now be obvious about the reality of suffering in our lives. As Jesus pointed out in John 16:33, we will have trouble in this world. It will surround us at times, and it may even engulf us. At times, we may be complicit in the cause of our troubles, and at other times it may simply arrive at our doorstep. This is the reality of life on planet earth.

Why Is Suffering So Common?

As Christians we take comfort in knowing that the source of our salvation is also the solution for our suffering. Even though that is true, it does nothing to explain why our world is continually bathed in suffering. We believe there is an answer to be had, and we find that answer in the temptation of Jesus.

Matthew 4 set the scene: Jesus, led by the Spirit, went to the desert to fast. There, Satan, hoping to catch Jesus in a weakened mental state, launched an all-out assault on Jesus as God in human form.

Attack 1:

> If you are the Son of God, tell these stones to become bread.
>
> Jesus: It is written: Man does not live on bread alone, but on every word that comes from the mouth of God. (Matthew 4:3–4)

Attack 2:

> If you are the Son of God, throw yourself down. For it is written: He will command his angels concerning you, and they will lift you up in their hand, so that you will not strike your foot against a stone.
>
> Jesus: It is written: Do not put the Lord your God to the test. (Matthew 4:6–7)

Attack 3:

> Again the devil took him to a very high mountain and showed him all the kingdoms of the world and their splendor. All this I will give you if you will bow down and worship me. (Matthew 4:8)

> Jesus: Away from me, Satan! For it is written: Worship the Lord your God and serve him only. (Matthew 4:10)

Note that Satan started out with "if you are the Son of God" in two of his attacks. Why would Satan say that? He knew full well who Jesus was, else why would he be tempting him? Satan was playing against the human temptation to answer an insult. Questioning Jesus's divinity was the ultimate insult, and Satan was banking on raising Jesus's dander so much that he would do something to demonstrate that he was indeed the Son of God. If Jesus responded, he demonstrated he is the Son of God, but he relinquished the claim to Messiah. Jesus would not take the bait.

Satan was now left with his last card. No more pretenses about pride and Jesus being the Son of God. No, Satan went for broke and took Jesus to a vantage point where he could see all that Satan could tempt him with. Namely, the kingdoms of the world. How could Satan offer something to Jesus if he really did not have the authority to do so? If Satan were not able to offer the kingdoms of the world, it would have been incredibly easy for Jesus to point that fact out. But, he did not do that.

Does Satan have dominion over the kingdoms of this world? In one sense, the answer is yes, and we see it in titles given to Satan: The prince of this world, as indicated in John 12:31, God of this world in 2 Corinthians 4:4, and prince of the power of the air in Ephesians 2:2.

Satan offered the kingdoms because he was currently the benefactor of a lease arrangement with the world and all it had to offer. There will come a time when the lease will be broken, and there will be a new heaven and a new earth as a result. That said, an ongoing result of sin is the disconnect of the soul, the body, and nature from God. We, therefore, should not be surprised at the amount of evil in the world when we consider that the current leaseholder is evil personified.

Sovereignty of God and Free Will of Man

You might question why Satan would go to the trouble of tempting Christ, or why Satan would tempt Job. If God is sovereign, wouldn't he already know the answers to Satan's questions (and any other question)? And if God is sovereign, how can man do something that God doesn't control?

Skeptics rightfully ask these types of questions. So do Christians. These are important questions because they get to the heart of the tension between God's sovereignty and man's free will. How is it possible for both to exist simultaneously? Or is it possible at all? Major contentions have developed within the church around this issue. Are Christians predestined to be Christians? Are nonbelievers predestined to hell as well?

We would like to take a moment to investigate these questions, and we will start by revisiting Job and the temptation of Christ. Did God know how Job would respond when put to the test? Absolutely. Was Job capable of not persevering through his trials? Absolutely. Did God know how Christ would respond when tempted? Absolutely. Was Christ's human nature capable of succumbing to the temptations of Satan? Absolutely. How can both be true? We turn to Psalm 139 for the answer.

> You have searched me Lord and you know me.
> You know when I sit and when I rise; you perceive
> my thoughts from afar. You discern my going out
> and my lying down; you are familiar with all my
> ways. Before a word is on my tongue you know it
> completely, O Lord. (Psalm 139:1–4)

The psalmist informed us that God knows all things, but the psalmist made it equally clear that God is not directing all things. Note that God knows when we sit and when we rise, but God allows those things to occur as a result of our will. God even knows what we will say, but he doesn't take the credit or blame for those words.

Psalm 139 made it clear that God can see the end from the beginning, as does Isaiah 46:10. This has huge implications for our lives. Yes, we do have the capacity to choose or reject God, and yes, God knows beforehand who will choose wisely. God's ability to see the end from the beginning is sometimes referred to as middle knowledge.[6] Because of middle knowledge, God can so order the world that every person of accountable age will have sufficient opportunity to choose to recognize their need for a savior. This squares well with scripture such as 2 Peter 3:9.

> The Lord is not slow in keeping his promise, as some understand slowness. Instead he is patient with you, not wanting anyone to perish, but everyone to come to repentance.

And with Romans 1:20:

> For since the creation of the world God's invisible qualities—his eternal power and divine nature—have been clearly seen, being understood from what has been made, so that people are without excuse.

While simultaneously reconciling with verses regarding predestination, such as Romans 8:29:

> For those God foreknew he also predestined to be conformed to the image of his Son, that he might be the firstborn among many brothers and sisters.

We suggest that God in his sovereignty arranges every person's condition such that it provides sufficient opportunity to accept his saving offer of grace through Jesus, via their free will. He wishes none to perish. Those who do not accept grace are without excuse. Those

---

[6] Middle knowledge is derived from the works of Luis de Molina. Alvin Plantinga has a thorough treatment of the subject in *God, Freedom, and Evil.*

that will accept the offer are foreknown by God in the same manner that he foreknows what a person will say before they say it. Since they are foreknown, they are therefore predestined.

We see no scriptural basis to suggest that God predestines anyone to hell. In fact, the opposite is true. Knowing this may prove very useful when talking to a skeptic about God's love or God's sovereignty. Unfortunately, some have made an argument that attempts to position God in a double predestination model. It is not surprising that these explanations often horrify a skeptic and make them question why they would ever want to worship a God that would do such a thing.[7]

Why We Can Trust a Sovereign God

Exodus 12 provided the Jewish nation directions for Passover observance. The observance was initiated to recall God's judgment upon Egypt for refusing to release the Jewish nation from bondage. Israel suffered under Egyptian rule for four hundred years (Genesis 15:13 and Acts 7:6) until Moses was designated as the earthly leader of the liberation effort. After several plagues, Pharaoh's neck remained stiff and he would not free the Israelites. In the final plague rendered by God, death visited the firstborn male of every family. Exception was granted to those houses who had marked their houses using specific instructions found in Exodus 12:1–14:

> The Lord said to Moses and Aaron in Egypt, "This month is to be for you the first month, the first month of your year. Tell the whole community of Israel that on the *tenth day* of this month each man is to take a lamb for his family, one for each household. If any household is too small for a whole lamb, they must share one with their nearest neighbor, having taken into account the

---

[7]   An excellent and succinct argument for this position has been offered by Dr. D. James Kennedy in his book *Evangelism Explosion*, 4th ed.

number of people there are. You are to determine the amount of lamb needed in accordance
with what each person will eat. The animals you
choose must be year-old males without defect,
and you may take them from the sheep or the
goats. Take care of them until the *fourteenth day*
of the month, when all the members of the community of Israel must slaughter them at twilight.
Then they are to take some of the blood and put
it on the sides and tops of the doorframes of the
houses where they eat the lambs. That same night
they are to eat the meat roasted over the fire,
along with bitter herbs, and bread made without
yeast. Do not eat the meat raw or boiled in water,
but roast it over a fire—with the head, legs,
and internal organs. Do not leave any of it till
morning; if some is left till morning, you must
burn it. This is how you are to eat it: with your
cloak tucked into your belt, your sandals on your
feet and your staff in your hand. Eat it in haste;
it is the Lord's Passover. On that same night I
will pass through Egypt and strike down every
firstborn of both people and animals, and I will
bring judgment on all the gods of Egypt. I am
the Lord. The blood will be a sign for you on the
houses where you are, and when I see the blood,
I will pass over you. No destructive plague will
touch you when I strike Egypt. This is a day you
are to commemorate; for the generations to come
you shall celebrate it as a festival to the Lord—a
lasting ordinance." (Emphasis added)

Lambs were selected on the tenth day of the month and were
sacrificed on the fourteenth. This was a lasting ordinance given to the
Jewish nation. The lambs were to be firstborns and without defect;
their blood identified the occupants of the house as God's chosen.

For millennia, Passover was observed as a reminder of the time when Israel was released from Egypt's bondage. One might think the point of Passover was to remind Jews, and by extension New Testament Christians, that God would deliver on his promises. Such believers would be partially right. We said partially right because that framework is retrospective, focusing on a past event.

For God, however, the first Passover was not his ultimate focus. Freeing a country from bondage is definitely a big deal, but it pales in comparison to freeing mankind from the bondage of sin. That occurred on another Passover, and it is truly amazing how many details of the account given to Moses and Aaron, so many years before, are fulfilled at the Last Supper and in the next few days.

The Passover

The following section draws heavily from *Chronological Aspects of the Life of Christ*,[8] a wonderful book authored by Harold H. Hoehner. It should be required reading for every Christian at some point in their walk. Shortly before the ultimate Passover, Jesus was working his way toward Jerusalem (John 11:55). According to John 12:1, Jesus arrived at Bethany six days before Passover was to commence; this would be a Saturday. That evening, Jesus was anointed at Simon the Leper's house (Matthew 26:6–13, Mark 14:3–9, and John 12:1–8). On Sunday, the next day, a large crowd came to Bethany to see Jesus (John 12:9–11).

John 12:12 then stated that the next day, Monday, Jesus made his triumphal entry into Jerusalem. If Hohner's view is correct, this would be the very day that the masses gathered in Jerusalem to celebrate Passover would have been selecting their lambs. This was lamb-selection day, the day that Jesus Christ, the Lamb of God who takes away the sins of the world (John 1:29), rode into Jerusalem on a borrowed donkey to fulfill the prophecy offered in Zechariah 9:9.

If Jesus arrived in Jerusalem on lamb-selection day, it is a straightforward analysis to determine that Jesus was slain on the day

---

8   Hoehner, Harold W. *Chronological Aspects of the Life of Christ*. Grand Rapids Mich.: Zondervan, 1977.

that the nation of Israel observed as an ordinance of God that a first-born male, without defect, was to be offered as a means to identify who actually belonged to God. And the means of identification was the blood of that male.

But there's more. According to scripture, Jesus died around 3:00 p.m. on Friday afternoon. What is significant about that time? According to the Jewish Encyclopedia of 1906, the Passover sacrifice is to begin at 3:00 p.m.[9] Before the individual sacrifices could be rendered, there would first be a national sacrifice offered by the high priest. He was to be spiritually and physically clean, and in case he was not, a rope was tied around his leg so he could be dragged from the inner temple in case he died as a result of his unclean condition. He would take the lamb selected as the national sacrifice, and at 3:00 p.m. he would offer its blood to God in the holy of holies as a means of atonement for Israel's collective sins. It was at that time that the real sacrifice was concluding on a hill called Golgotha, when Jesus uttered his last living words (before he resurrected) at 3:00 p.m.: "It is finished" (John 19:30).

Providing *the* Passover Lamb on lamb-selection day was surely no accident. Sacrificing *the* Passover Lamb at the moment when Israel's high priest was sacrificing a Passover Lamb was surely no accident.

The connection between the Passover of Exodus and the final Passover of the New Testament shows clearly and conclusively that God's clock may grind slowly but it grinds inexorably. God is sovereign, and therefore, he and he alone is able to orchestrate events so that all things work for good for those who love the Lord (Romans 8:28).

Before time began, God knew how he would solve the dilemma that man created. Man made a mess of paradise, but God provided a solution. Man left God deliberately and by doing so declared himself God, but the real God made a way to mediate for that blasphemy. Man never could attain holiness, but God made a way for holiness

---

[9] The entire Jewish Encyclopedia of 1906 may be found at http://jewishencyclopedia.com.

to be imparted. Man could never atone for his sins, so God provided grace.

These truths are immutable. They are far more relevant than your bank account, your societal status, or your latest checkup. They are more relevant than a cancer diagnosis or even the death of a loved one. These truths are ultimate because they transcend this world and its troubles. To be possessed by God is to be totally secure in this world and for all eternity. No wonder Paul asked in Romans 8:31: "If God is for us who can be against us?"

Further Reflection

Central theme: This attack on God (i.e., the existence of evil), in our opinion, is one of the most dangerous. It must be answered and answered well if the skeptic's understandable concerns will be addressed. Maybe even more important, it must be answered well if we as Christians are not to be doomed to live in constant doubt about whether God is really there and whether he really cares.

Reflective Activities

1. Does the presence of evil provide evidence that God is not all-powerful or all-loving? What evidence counters this claim?
2. Was evil created?
3. How might God's sovereignty and man's free will both be realities?
4. We have argued in this chapter that God's sovereignty and his nature require that every person have a sufficient opportunity for salvation. Do you agree with our position?
5. Why were Job's friends so insistent on blaming Job for his problems?
6. We have argued in this chapter that our response to trouble takes precedence over the problem itself. Do you agree with our position? If so, what are the implications for a believer?

Chapter 6

Prepared to Give an Account for the Hope You Have

Then you will know the truth, and the truth shall set you free.[1]

We hope that we have demonstrated that the Christian faith is not blind. It is based upon fact and reason because God has been generous in the clues he left for anyone who might believe.

All that said, we find ourselves increasingly in hostile waters from the world's perspective. Consider the following online post with a religious theme as a typical example.[2]

- Religion demands the removal of all logic and reason. No thanks, I like being sane.
- Faith in a magical sky fairy? You prove my point.
- We don't laugh at religion, only at its followers.

We could go on, but this short discussion thread distinctly documents the gulf between skeptics and believers. We are painting with

---

[1] The words of Jesus as recorded in John 8:32.
[2] It has often been said that death and taxes are the only certainties in life. We can now add a third: The inevitable launching of insults by both sides whenever an article with Christian overtones is posted online.

a broad brush here, but we maintain that the premise we present is true more often than not. Namely, skeptics tend to criticize our beliefs from their head, and believers tend to defend beliefs from their heart.

It is also true that many skeptics criticize our beliefs from a perspective of pain and suffering. They may say that even if there is a God, he is not worth my time. We want to discuss these lines of attack separately since they are so different, and we begin with the first scenario.

Knowledge: Necessary but Often Lacking

We are certain there is truth to the generalization that skeptics attack from the head (and as we will see shortly, perhaps from the heart as well). Therefore, it is imperative that churches adapt strategies that accentuate the rationality of the Christian faith while still maintaining the emphasis upon spiritual growth and maturity.

If we in the church expect to attract skeptics, it seems like we will need to appreciate the mind-set the skeptic is likely to bring. Given the derision for our beliefs that is found among many skeptics, it is to be expected that we must first implement a practical approach to explaining not only what we believe but, just as importantly, why we believe it. If we cannot answer the "why," a skeptic is almost certain to dismiss the "what."

So how do we proclaim the good news to those who are not particularly interested in hearing it? First, by becoming grounded in our beliefs. We really need to know and communicate a rational argument for the existence of God and the divinity of Christ. We also better be prepared to speak to someone about how God can exist in a world inundated with pain and suffering.

This is a first step, but it is not the final step. If we internalize the truths of God and the Bible, it is hard to see how they would not be transformative. Said another way, since we are new creations in Christ, we should behave that way. God has made that doable for us by providing his Spirit to indwell us, to live with us and to produce fruit through us.

If we as believers hold the upper hand in these matters, why are we so reluctant to engage discussions with skeptics? Our conclusion is that the reluctance stems mostly from a lack of appreciation for how well-grounded our cases are for the four pillars of Christianity.

Although we hold credible answers for the difficult questions posed by skeptics, we do not tend to access them as often as we should.

This is a major impediment to the proclamation of the gospel. Furthermore, the lack of appreciation for the soundness of our beliefs is likely having major consequences in churches and their members. For example, it has often been noted that the divorce rate for Christians and non-Christians is essentially the same.[3] How can this be if the transformative power of the Holy Spirit is guiding our marriages? How can it be that churches fail to add a single member in a year? Or that so many churches are closing their doors?

Perhaps a major reason for all these tragedies is the lack of appreciation for the pillars of our faith? If we as believers are absolutely convinced that God exists, Jesus is divine, and that he denied death and provides a means for us to do so as well. If we as believers are absolutely convinced that God exists, Jesus is divine, and that he conquered death and provides a means for us to do so as well, and if we are convinced that the solution to a world so plagued by pain and suffering is a relationship with the one true God who promises we will one day be removed from pain and suffering forever, why isn't that translating into results? The forces that drove twelve men to change their world are still available to us today, and the God who created this universe is still alive and well. Maybe, just maybe,

---

[3] https://www.barna.com/research/new-marriage-and-divorce-statistics-released. The Barna Group tracked divorce rates for Christians and non-Christians. The good news is that the often reported 50 percent failure rate for Christian marriages is a myth. Barna reported the general divorce rate is 33 percent and notes that marriages of proclaiming Christians had a divorce rate of 32 percent. If one is looking for "good news," those who identified as evangelicals had a divorce rate of 28 percent.

if churches emphasized why we believe as much as what we believe it might make a difference? Maybe?

Good Things but Not Sufficient Things

Churches are sensitive to the challenges we just noted, but we are afraid the strategies often employed to meet these challenges are hamstrung because their focus is on peripheral changes rather than core truths. In an effort to attract new members, churches have retooled their delivery strategies. To reach a new generation, new songs are sung. To increase socialization, coffee shops spring up. To demonstrate the inclusiveness of the gospel, pastors dress casually. To enhance personal accountability, small groups are emphasized.

To a skeptic, these efforts may make the church appear contemporary, inviting, and interested in fostering friendships. Good things all, but none of these accoutrements are sufficient to convince someone (anyone) that the church possesses truth.

James Emery White tackled the problem of the rising percentage of people who no longer consider church important in his book *Rise of the Nones*.[4] White argued that churches a few years ago erred when they moved too far toward a "let's go and be" at the expense of "come and see." Friendliness, children's ministry, music, buildings, and the importance of the visual were identified as crucial for a church to be sustainable.

White may be correct about the cultural attractiveness of these strategies, but it begs this question: What is the value of an attractive church that cannot or does not answer ultimate questions? That question is not posed to bash White or his book, but the fact that it can be asked indicates the lack of attention that is provided to addressing the four pillars of Christianity by one of the most popular books on reimagining the experience of church in print today.

Certainly there are some who are enticed to church because of these attracting strategies. Ultimately though, every person who has ever attended and will ever attend a church wants to know whether

---

[4] White, James Emery. *The Rise of the Nones: Understanding and Reaching the Religiously Unaffiliated*. Grand Rapids: Baker Books, 2014.

the whole exercise is a charade, or whether there really is a God that provided a means for sinful man to be reconciled with him for all eternity. For whatever reason, this universal truth is under recognized and too often ignored by far too many churches and efforts to revision churches.

As we have continuously asserted, the church tends to assume that our truths are accepted, and we have seen the crippling results of this flawed conclusion. Unfortunately, a lackadaisical approach to our truths is directly correlated to the continued demise of the church's influence and indeed its credibility in the eyes of skeptics.

We believe that, on any given Sunday pews are full of hopers, i.e., people who have no way to validate that what they believe is in fact true. They feel the presence of God, but they also wonder whether the feeling is self-created. They pray to a living God, but they wonder if they are speaking to themselves. They wonder about their salvation because they wonder about whether anything they believe is believable.

If this is the case, no amount of environmental improvements will fill the void created by doubt. A church can be friendly, inviting, and contemporary, yet still do little to assuage the doubts of the believer in the pew. And if the church is not easing the doubts of the believer, it should be all too clear what is happening in the skeptic's mind.

Many churches follow White's conclusions, focusing on the experience of worship at the expense of the defense of the message. Strong words. But how else to explain the repeated attestations by "grizzled" believers we alluded to in chapter 1? How else to explain how they have never been exposed to the core rationales for the Christian faith in their respective churches? If a believer does not have a grasp of the rational basis for their faith, how do they grow during worship? Most importantly, what are they really worshipping? Their plight seems to be more similar than dissimilar to the hopers we just described.

The failure to build a strong foundational argument for a case would be fatal in a courtroom, a boardroom, a family, or virtually anywhere else. That said, the institution that guards the most important truth of all is often failing to build its case. The loss of cultural influence and relevancy the church is experiencing today is due to many factors, but none carry more weight than the failure to adequately explain why we know what we believe is true.

It is intuitive to say there are two reasons people attend church. Either they are looking for God or they have found God. This may be intuitive, but it is also fatally simplistic. Many are attending out of habit, others are attending out of fear, hedging bets as it were. Still others are wrestling with many of the doubts we have articulated, while others are looking for a reason to believe.

We could go on but you get the point. There are as many reasons people are attending church as there are people in the pews.[5] The glue that should bind them all should be the commonly held beliefs about the existence of God, the divinity of Christ, the reality of Christ's resurrection, and a proper perspective on pain and suffering, but unfortunately, that is just not the case.

In his book, White correctly noted that churches are composed primarily of folks who are already churched. Said another way, churches keep trading church members and typically are not terribly effective at reaching new members—at least not new members who tend to approach Christianity from a skeptical perspective. We are recycling Christians, and for the most part, are failing to reach the skeptic and the doubter.

Knowledge and Application: Both Are Necessary and Neither Stands Alone

There is another situation that the church must do a better job of addressing. The reality of pain and suffering is often seen by the skeptic or cynic as game, set, and match when it comes to accepting Christianity as rational. This problem involves both the head and the heart. It is not enough to explain suffering; we must be willing to engage it if we are to have any shot at credibility.

---

[5] http://www.pewresearch.org/fact-tank/2013/09/13/what-surveys-say-about-worship-attendance-and-why-some-stay-home. The Pew Research Center has an extensive bank of research on the trends associated with church attendance. An example of their research can be found at this link.

Nothing replaces a friend that stands with you when times are particularly bad. Job's buddies were very good at providing rationales for his anguish, but they were no help at all. Telling the woman who had a miscarriage that it was God's will and then walking away causes more problems than it solves. The head cannot be separated from the heart in God's economy.

In Auburn, Alabama, a group of internationals met weekly for language classes. Friendships developed and moved beyond the Wednesday meetings. A family from South Korea began meeting with Wade and his family. Eventually, the man revealed he was mad at God because his mother, a Christian, had died from cancer even though there had been fervent prayer for healing.

Time passed, and eventually the family was to return to South Korea. The last night in Auburn, they were hosted for dinner by Wade and his wife. It is reasonable to assume they were the only South Koreans in America eating seafood gumbo, but that is another story. As the man, his wife, and their three-year-old child left the house for the last time, the gentleman turned and gave his last good-bye: "Many people have talked to us about love, but you have shown it. We have much to think about."

Aha, you say. That story demonstrates that he never questioned why we believe, but here is the rest of the story. A few weeks prior to that encounter, a group of internationals were sitting at a table eating dinner before the language classes began. One turned to Wade and said, "I want to believe in God but I need proof."

"What kind of proof would you like?"

"I want to see that saltshaker move."

It was pointed out at that point that there were stories of folks being raised from the dead and people being healed that, although seen, did not serve as proof. In other words, if that were the burden of proof expected, it was not going to be reached. But when asked if a rational explanation for the existence of God was something he would like to see, he enthusiastically said he would.

A week later, at a Saturday BBQ, there were about seventy-five internationals. They were there to play table tennis, eat BBQ, and hang out. They had been told that if they wanted to, they could stay for a presentation on the rational existence of God. Everyone stayed. The room was jammed with doctoral and postdoctoral students, along with their spouses.

They went through a rational explanation for the existence of God and asked for questions. One remarked that Wade should write a book, and everyone agreed that the presentation offered a strong defense of God's existence.

Our South Korean friend was there at that presentation. He had begun to weigh the validity of the arguments, and he was no longer willing to dismiss God as an artificial construct. Now he had to wrestle with how the Christian God could allow his mother to suffer and die.

It was clear in his particular case that the rationality of the message and the expression of love that comes from God's grace were both necessary ingredients for him to renew his own struggle to determine ultimate reality. The rationality of the belief would have been insufficient without the expression of love that accompanies a life in Christ, and indeed, the expression of love would have been insufficient without the rational basis for its source.

We return now to a now familiar scripture. It has served as the starting point for this book, and it is a reminder to us all that we cannot separate the head and the heart when it comes to God.

> But in your hearts revere Christ as Lord. Always be prepared to give an answer to everyone who asks you to give the reason for the hope that you have. But do this with gentleness and respect, keeping a clear conscience, so that those who speak maliciously against your good behavior in Christ may be ashamed of their slander. (1 Peter 3:15–16)

"Always be prepared to give an answer" is another way of saying "Be able to tell people why you believe." Do this gently and with humility so that people cannot slander you because of your good behavior. People should know we are changed by Christ because we should be broadcasting this fact to a skeptical world that is trying just as hard as we are to make sense of what they see around them.

The head and the heart at work. This is how the church is designed to operate. We hope our thoughts will serve to remind Christians everywhere that we do not have to shrink when our beliefs are challenged. So what now?

Further Reflection

Central theme: If we cannot answer why we believe, a skeptic is almost certain to dismiss what we believe.

Reflective Activities

1. Are churches responding appropriately to the rising skepticism they face?
2. In your opinion, do churches tend to assume the average church attendee is well versed in the pillars of the Christian faith?
3. Is there a strong likelihood that many attending church today do so hoping the Christian faith is true instead of knowing that to be the case?

Chapter 7

A Call to Action for Churches

> More and more churches are relying on market-
> ing strategy to sell the church. That philosophy is
> the result of bad theology. It assumes that if you
> package the gospel right, people will get saved.[1]

Jesus told Peter the gates of hell would not prevail against his church. If we know anything, it is that Jesus can be trusted. The church is God's primary means of spreading the Gospel and matur-ing the believer. Indeed, the former will not take place without the latter. Additionally, the church is a sanctuary for the wounded and the displaced. In other words, the church is a place where the head, the heart, and the hands are all engaged.

We believe the previous chapter makes it clear that churches are very sensitive to the hands and the heart, but not quite as focused on the head. We also believe that this shortcoming is a significant hin-drance in furthering the cause of Christ. With this in mind, we now turn to a set of recommendations that every church should carefully gauge to see if there might be cause to incorporate some or all the following:

---

[1] https://www.gty.org/library/articles/A163/Gimme-That-Showtime-Religion.
Here are John MacArthur's musings on this subject.

Every Church Should Provide Members with an Adequate Base of Foundational Knowledge

1. Believers need information.

The focus here is on the believer's well-being. Changing oil and filters, rotating tires, and performing tune-ups at the correct mileage intervals are necessary to keep cars running optimally. By the same token, knowledge maintenance is necessary to ensure that believers are equipped to fend off the attacks that are being generated at an ever increasing rate. These attacks tend to originate from science, history, or morality, and Christians should be able to recognize them and deal with them. Like cars, churches should have a "service engine soon" option that allows believers to deal with doubts, acquire knowledge, and ultimately live confidently that their faith is not blind and their hope is not whimsy.

As we just noted, skeptical arguments are almost certain to come from science, history, or morality. Christians should feel confident in dealing with these issues, and toward this end, churches should provide regular presentations on the existence of God, the divinity of Christ, the evidence for the resurrection, and the Christian response to evil.[2]

Included with this book are reflective questions for each of these topics. Churches may choose to use these resources or develop their own, but in either case, it is important that the effort be provided high priority on the calendar.

2. Believers need to know how to share their knowledge with grace and humility.

We have argued that there has been a not-so-subtle shift in the culture that makes sharing your story very difficult. First, the church

---

[2] We find it remarkable that so much is assumed about foundational beliefs for church attendees. Many churches hold 101 courses, but they often focus on what the church believes about certain denominational positions rather than why (and how) the whole enterprise of Christianity can be rationally defended.

has not been terribly effective in guarding its own intellectual property. As a result, many skeptics now assume that Christianity and superstition are synonymous.

Second, there is a loss of credibility because of this, and the church is now placed in a defensive mode where any efforts to evangelize are met with cynicism. Third, the culture is becoming increasingly secular, and there is a growing view that religion has no place in daily conversation.[3]

All these factors mitigate against a testimony based primarily upon personal experience. That type of witness is likely to be seen as an irrational attestation to something that is not real, the motives as questionable, and the whole effort as intrusive. Recently over lunch, a friend of ours relayed how he had tried to speak to his neighbor about God. He asked his neighbor about his walk and the neighbor said his walk was fine. The friend replied he meant how was his walk with God? The neighbor responded, "God who?"

Ouch. Hard to go anywhere from there. We need to recognize that this type of response is no longer uncommon. If we start from the supposition that God is understood to be a reality, we are quite likely going to be shocked at how quickly that supposition is challenged. We should also be aware that as general church attendance declines, fewer and fewer people have been exposed to Sunday school and sermons where biblical stories have been retold.

As a result, the level of biblical illiteracy is on a steady uptick. People who are biblically illiterate are not likely to have any interest in pursuing the claims that the Bible makes. For the most part, it is correct to assume the illiteracy is a result of apathy or rejection of the Bible altogether. Asking this type of skeptic about their walk with the Lord is just about guaranteed to be met with derision.

So how, then, do we make our case? First, we are most likely to gain an audience when we are speaking to someone we know. We are all bombarded with spam and robocalls, and we have all become

---

[3] As documented in the introduction, there is a disturbing trend in the public's rising skepticism of the credibility of religion. This bad news is exacerbated by up to a 50 percent exaggeration in actual church attendance.

accustomed to quickly screening what we wish to hear and what we wish to delete. If we are not careful, we will become "human spam" that becomes a nuisance before we ever get to the heart of a conversation.

Most people are not really comfortable doing this though. Speaking to someone you know about what you believe can seem a little disingenuous. No one likes to be invited to dinner to find out it was really an excuse to present an investment scheme. So, too, with the skeptic. If there is a feeling that the whole conversation is contrived it may already be on borrowed time. This problem is not unique to our current time. In fact, Peter anticipated the problem.

> But in your hearts revere Christ as Lord. Always be prepared to give an answer to everyone who asks you to give the reason for the hope that you have. But do this with gentleness and respect. (1 Peter 3:15)

People do not generally ask strangers to give a reason for the hope that they have. Peter is suggesting that people see something different in us, and they will want to know what it is. That means they know us, and they not only know us, but they know us well enough that they want to know the motives behind our behavior.

Returning to the previous example, it is clear that the neighbors have known each other for quite some time. So far, so good. The problem is the neighbor did not ask to be critiqued. If he would have said, "I don't think I'm right with God, what do I need to do?" it would have been very appropriate to take that invitation and answer with gentleness and respect. Bringing the question to the table without those dynamics colors the whole conversation, as we saw.

We are not suggesting the neighbor should remain in stoic silence until an opportunity to respond with gentleness and respect arises. If he did that, there would likely never be an opportunity to be heard. We are suggesting that initiating a conversation of this nature has a greater chance at success if the skeptic is asked to critique what we believe rather than having to defend what they believe.

This is not far removed from the bulk of everyday conversation that everyone engages in. We routinely explain why we like one car over another, why we choose to eat at a particular restaurant, and so forth. Explaining why we believe there is a God, why we believe Jesus is the Son of God, why we believe in the physical resurrection of Christ, and why we believe there is a Christian perspective to suffering that explains how evil and God can both exist is far different than telling our story.

In the right circumstances, our story is not what we say but what we do. Our story in this case is that our lives become a testimony that prompts someone to ask why we behave the way we do. Now we get to give a reason for the hope that we have.

That will not be the norm for many of us though. In many cases, we will be speaking with someone that we simply do not know well enough for that type of a question to arise. That does not mean we cannot be ambassadors for Christ, but it does mean we will likely need to adapt our conversation to a place where we ask someone to critique what we believe.

However, if we do that, we had better be prepared to give rationale for our beliefs or the conversation will serve to heighten the skeptic's conviction that the whole "Jesus thing" is nothing more than a personal claim to truth instead of an absolute standard of reality.

3. Churches need to provide practical training on how to speak to a skeptic.

Churches have diligently covered how to witness to others, but these efforts typically assume a willing participant. That is, they assume that you are witnessing to someone who is actively seeking, or at the very least is open to considering your personal testimony. There has been little attention given to reversing the conversation and allowing the skeptic to question the "whys" of our faith. That needs to change.

There is a desperate need for churches to provide opportunities for their congregations to learn how to speak intelligently about their belief in God, the divinity of Christ, the evidence for the resurrection, and the Christian perspective on suffering and evil. Training of this nature should allow members to practice in real-life scenarios with people who can skillfully challenge the argument that is laid out by the apologist.[4]

Practice, perseverance, practice. This process builds confidence in what you want to say and how you want to say it. It allows for self-analysis about ways to confidently respond when our beliefs are challenged (and they most assuredly will be challenged), and it is based on real-world expectations.

4. Churches should focus on the essentials.

The existence of God, the divinity of Christ, the evidence for the resurrection, and the Christian perspective on evil or suffering are the big issues.[5]

If a skeptic wants to argue the sun cannot go backward, for example, it might be a good time to note that he or she is arguing against the possibility of a miracle (an argument from science). Since that is the case, it would be useful to investigate the wildest miracle claim of all, the resurrection of a man three days dead, to see if it holds water. If that miracle can be verified, the other miracles are certainly within the power of an omniscient and omnipotent God.

If the skeptic contends that the Bible is a book written by men, full of errors, it might be useful to point out the prophecies about Jesus and their fulfillment in the New Testament. Of course, this will lead to other discussions, but that is precisely the point. Now we are having discussions about what we believe rather than disparaging the skeptic for what they do not believe.

It should be obvious that these types of conversations will be fluid and will require a foundational knowledge base and an ability to speak clearly to the points that are being made. This is why churches

---

[4] This necessity is likely one of the most overlooked in churches today. We are aware of several instances of poorly prepared apologists having their arguments tossed back at them, because many have said so at our presentations.

[5] The further we travel from the fundamentals of the faith, the more likely we are to create a hazard or diversion for belief.

need to get directly involved in training programs to help their members develop strong apologetic skills.

5. Churches should consider working together to host apologetic conferences and speakers.

The topics we have covered are *foundational*, not *denominational*. The willingness of churches to band together in the common cause of educating their members would have numerous advantages. Small churches simply cannot afford this type of enterprise, but working with other churches would introduce an adequate economy of scale so that even the smallest church's members could benefit.

Also, these efforts could create synergy between churches, something that is far too rare in today's world. The ability of churches to work beyond denominational lines is going to be essential if individual churches are going to realize their true potential. Ecclesiastes 4:12 comes to mind, and although the context is about people, the same principle applies if you substitute "churches."

> Though one may be overpowered, two can defend themselves. A cord of three strands is not quickly broken.

6. Churches should create training teams to assist other churches.

There will be times when, for whatever reason, churches may not be able to pool their resources. In these cases, churches that have the means should develop teams of trainers and coaches to assist other churches in their efforts to build a foundational knowledge base for their congregations. This means that you need apologists who can hit the road. It also means that you need teams that can follow up with the real-world training that is vital to producing confident witnesses for Christ.

In today's world, the church operates far too often as a single entity.[6] This type of exercise could be a launching point for churches to merge their talents and strengths for the single cause of Christ.

7.   Churches should talk about these topics regularly.

Foundational pillars of the faith should continually be affirmed and honored. It is incumbent upon the church to announce to skeptics and members alike what our core beliefs are and why we know them to be true. Repeating these truths and their defenses, regularly, is the primary means of ensuring that they are passed to the next generation.

The Future Church

Tremendous amounts of time and talent are being expended on reinventing churches to negotiate the shifting cultural sands. Churches are working diligently to be viewed as warm and open environments where people can find friends and refuge. This progress should take with it the never changing argument for the truth of our message. The message is always more important than the medium used to disseminate it. The way we conduct church is simply a tool to convey universal and timeless truths about the veracity of the Christian worldview.

The message too often seems to be lost in translation. The church of the future will need to recognize that it is facing multiple challenges on simultaneous fronts. It seems that there has been a tendency to attack these challenges in silos (i.e., Sunday school for youth, contemporary services for Generation X and Y, traditional services for the gray hairs, and on and on).

These are all tools to carry the message. Yet as we have seen throughout this book, there is a pretty good chance that the message

---

[6]   An unfortunate irony about God's church is the incredible lack of economy of scale. The opportunity to work hand in hand with other churches on large issues is something we do not do very well.

being delivered by these tools does not adequately prepare believers to address attacks upon the pillars of our faith.

The next generation of believers will be challenged to reclaim ground that has been lost in the intellectual battle with nonbelievers. We cannot afford to remain passively silent while atheists work zealously to undermine our credibility. And we certainly cannot assume it is someone else's responsibility in the church to provide the defenses. Finally, we cannot afford to get caught up in details about how we deliver the message at the expense of the message itself.

So what exactly is the message? It is simply this: The God of the Bible exists, Jesus Christ is divine, he has risen from the grave, and he and he alone provides a solution to the pain and suffering we all feel in this life. Accepting these pillars and permitting Jesus to provide for an eternal relation with the Father is the ultimate end for this message. Defending the four pillars is the mission, and we pray this book has contributed toward that end.

Further Reflection

Central theme: The topics we have covered are foundational, not denominational. Foundational pillars of the faith should continually be affirmed and honored.

Reflective Activities

1. What do you see as the biggest threats to the church's ability to meet the challenges we have covered?
2. Where do you see the church in ten years?
3. From your perspective, has the church adequately defended its four foundational pillars from skeptical attacks?
4. Do you feel more confident about your faith and your ability to express the evidence for your faith to others?

Bibliography

Alexander Vilenkin, *Many Worlds in One: The Search for Other Universes* (New York: Hill & Wang, 2006), 176.

Antony Flew, with Roy Abraham Varghese, *There is A God: How the World's Most Notorious Atheist Changed His Mind* (New York: Harper Collins, 2007), 72.

C.S. Lewis, *Mere Christianity* (New York: Harper Collins, 1952), 54-56.

Colin Hemer, *The Book of Acts in the Setting of Hellenistic History* (Tubingen: J.C.B. Mohr, 1989).

George Smoot, *Wrinkles in Time* (New York: Avon Books, 1993), 283.

Harold Hoehner, *Chronological Aspects of the Life of Christ* (Grand Rapids: Zondervan, 1977).

Henry F. Schaefer, *Science and Christianity, 2nd Edition: Conflict or Coherence?* (Athens, Georgia: The Apollos Trust, 2013), 64-65.

Henry Margeneau, and Roy Abraham Varghese (Ed), *Cosmos, Bios, Theos: Scientists Reflect on Sciemce, God, and the Origins of the Universe, Life, and Homo Sapiens* (Peru, Illinois: Open Court Publishing, 1992), 82.

James Emery White, *The Rise of the Nones* (Grand Rapids: Baker Books, 2014).

John Lennox, *God and Stephen Hawking* (United Kingdom: Lions Publishing, 2011), 36.

Lisa Grossman, *New Science,* https://www.newscientist.com/article/mg21328474.400-why-physicists-cant-avoid-a-creation-event/

Martin Rees, *Just Six Numbers: The Deep Forces that Shape the Universe* (New York: Basic Books, 2000).

N. T. Wright, *The Resurrection of the Son of God* (Minneapolis: Fortress Press, 2003).

N. T. Wright, *The Self-Revelation of God in Human History: A Dialogue on Jesus with N. T. Wright.* In Antony Flew and Roy Abraham Varghese, *There is A God: How the world's most notorious atheist changed his mind.* (New York: Harper, Collins, 2007).

Norman L. Geisler, *Baker Encyclopedia of Christian Apologetics* (Grand Rapids: Baker Academic, 2006).

Peter Kreeft and Ronald K. Tacelli, *Handbook of Christian Apologetics* (Downer's Grove, Illinois: Intervarsity Press, 1994).

Pirsen A. Birgsen, *The Gospel According to the Jesus Seminar,* http://www.veritas-ucsb.org/library/pearson/seminar/js1.html on 10.5.16

R.C. Sproul, *Not a Chance: The Myth of Chance in Modern Science and Cosmology* (Grand Rapids: Baker Books, 1994).

Raphael Patai, *The Messiah Texts* (Avon Books, 1979), p vii.

Ravi Zacharias, *The End of Reason: A Response to the New Atheists* (Grand Rapids, Michigan: Zondervan, 2008), 37.

Robert Jastrow, *God and the Astronomers* (New York: W.W. Norton, 1978), 116.

Stephen Hawking, *A Brief History of Time* (New York: Bantam Books, 1988), 140-141.

Stephen Hawking, and Leonard Mlodinow, *The Grand Design* (New York: Bantam Books, 2010), 180.

Timothy Keller, *The Reason for God: Belief in an Age of Skepticism* (New York: Dutton, 2008).

"The Moon, the Tides, and Why Neil deGrasse Tyson is Colbert's God," January 20, 2011, The Science Network, video

William Lane Craig, *On Guard: Defending Your Faith with Reason and Precision* (Colorado Springs: David C. Cook Publishing, 2010).

About the Authors

Wade Smith is a career educator and holds a PhD in educational research. He has worked as a teacher, administrator, superintendent, and professor. His path to accepting Christ was directly influenced by the rational evidence that Christ is divine and he resurrected from the dead. Wade and his wife, Linda, have two grown daughters, Christie and LeAnn. Cars and motorcycles are his hobbies. His passion is presenting a gentle defense of Christianity to those who are wrestling with whether or not this thing called Christianity could possibly be true.

Kevin McKee is the lead pastor at the Chapel on the Campus, Baton Rouge, Louisiana. He has served as a pastor for many different ages. He became a Christian through the relational ministry of Young Life at sixteen. He received his theological education at Dallas Theological Seminary and Gordon-Conwell Theological Seminary. Kevin and his wife, Mary, have four children—Monica, Stewart, Joanna, and Lincoln. Fishing and spending time with the family are his hobbies. His passion is to tell others about the love and grace of Jesus.